D1444528

PICTURE IT!

COVER PHOTO: Editorial Photocolor Archives

COVER DESIGN: Joan Croom

PAGE DESIGN: Joan Croom

ILLUSTRATIONS: Richard Toglia

CONSULTANT: John Dumicich, American Language Program
                 New York University

10 9 8 7 6 5 4

Published by
Regents Publishing Company, Inc.
2 Park Avenue
New York, N.Y. 10016

Printed in the United States of America

ISBN 0-88345-413-0

INTRODUCTION

Picture It! Sequences for Conversation is designed for adolescent and adult students of English as a second language. It is intended for those who have had a basic introduction to English but need further practice in talking about essential, everyday experiences. The book can be used with any basic text and is a useful complement to any beginning or intermediate ESL course which follows a notional/functional or grammar-oriented syllabus.

Picture It! is divided into 15 self-contained units. Each unit consists of four parts. First there is a series of 32 PICTURES which form the basis for oral practice. These are followed by four sequences of BASE SENTENCES relating to the pictures. After that, there are four sets of PRACTICE EXERCISES, and finally a CONVERSATION section with lead-in questions.

By using the Table of Contents, you can choose the topic you wish to have students talk about, the grammatical item you wish them to practice, or the language function you wish them to perform. The units can be presented in sequence, or you may skip around. Units one through five discuss present activities using the simple present tense and the present continuous tense. Units six through ten present past activities using the simple past and the *used to* past. Units 11 through 15 employ imperatives and modals such as *should, might,* and *will.*

The PICTURES provide students with a visual context for the unit and stimulate interest. The BASE SENTENCES supply a sample verbal description to go along with the pictures. The PRACTICE EXERCISES provide a grammatical focus and allow for reinforcement of a particular grammar point. The CONVERSATION section provides questions to stimulate discussion. It helps students review the material they have just covered and apply it to themselves. Finally, the ANSWER KEY at the back of the book allows students to do individual work outside of class.

TABLE OF CONTENTS

TO THE TEACHER

TO THE TEACHER

Begin each lesson by giving students some time to become familiar with the situation presented in the pictures. Work with one eight-picture sequence at a time. First have students look at each picture as you read the corresponding sentence sequence. You may wish to repeat this step and answer student questions at this point. When you are sure that students understand what each picture represents, have them repeat each sentence after you while they continue to look at the pictures.

Next have students open their books to the written sequence which corresponds to the pictures they have just looked at. Have students repeat each sentence after you while following along in their books. At this point you may wish to have some students read aloud. Answer any further student questions at this time. When students have mastered one eight-picture sequence, repeat the above procedures for the other three sequences in each unit.

After introducing all four sentence sequences, go on to the Practice section. Throughout this section the teacher reads a *cue* sentence, and the student responds by transforming that sentence according to the instructions. (Teacher cues for Practice 1 of each unit are found in Sequence 1 of that unit.) For instance, in Unit 1, Practice 1, you read the instructions: "Change *Erik* to *I*." Then read the first sentence from Sequence 1: "Erik wakes up at seven o'clock." The student you call on replies by changing *Erik* to *I*: "I wake up at seven o'clock." Then you read the second sentence of Sequence 1 and call on another student to make the transformations. (Correct transformations are listed in the Answer Key at the back of the book.) Continue this technique until all eight sentences have been transformed. Then go on to Practice 2.

Teacher cues for Practices 2, 3, and 4 are listed within the practice itself. You will not need to refer back to the Sequences for these Practices. For example, in Unit 1, Practice 2, read the instructions: "End each sentence with *every morning*." Then read the cue sentence after the word *Example*: "I shave with an electric razor." The student you call on replies by adding *every morning*: "I shave with an electric razor every morning." All teacher cues are given in these practice exercises, but only the first student transformation is listed here. The rest of the transformations are in the Answer Key at the back of the book. Continue reading the other cue sentences in Practice 2 and calling on students to make the required transformations. Then use the same technique with Practice 3 and Practice 4.

When you have completed all Practices, introduce the Conversation section. Begin by having individuals answer the questions in one or two sentences. If the sentences are different from those in the book, you may wish to write some of them on the blackboard. Encourage students to talk freely about the topic and to make connections with their own lives. You can help by supplying vocabulary and correcting grammar when necessary. This part of the lesson is vital in helping learners discover useful vocabulary and in helping them gain confidence in their speaking ability.

Any of the practices supplied in a given unit can be applied to any sequence of eight pictures in that unit. For instance, if your students need more practice with the negative, you could ask them to apply Practice 3 (*Change each sentence to the negative.*) to all four sequences of pictures in Unit 1.

The pictures can be used for a variety of other purposes. You can open the book to any two-page spread and ask students to make up their own sentences about the pictures they see. You can then write some of these sentences on the board as the basis of a writing lesson. Later you could read these sentences aloud as a dictation.

Another use of the pictures is as the basis for a ten or fifteen-line story based on one sequence. You can write the story and have enough copies made for each student in your class. After students have read the passage and asked questions, you might give a 10-question reading comprehension quiz.

As you can see, *Picture It!* can be used in many different ways. It can supply material for oral practice, reading lessons, or writing exercises. With 32 pictures and 32 base sentences in each unit, the possibilities for creative teacher use are endless.

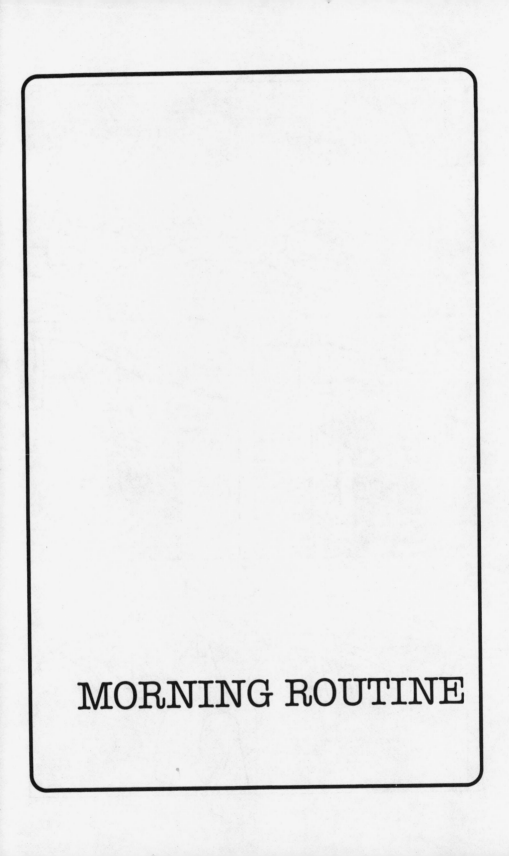

MORNING ROUTINE

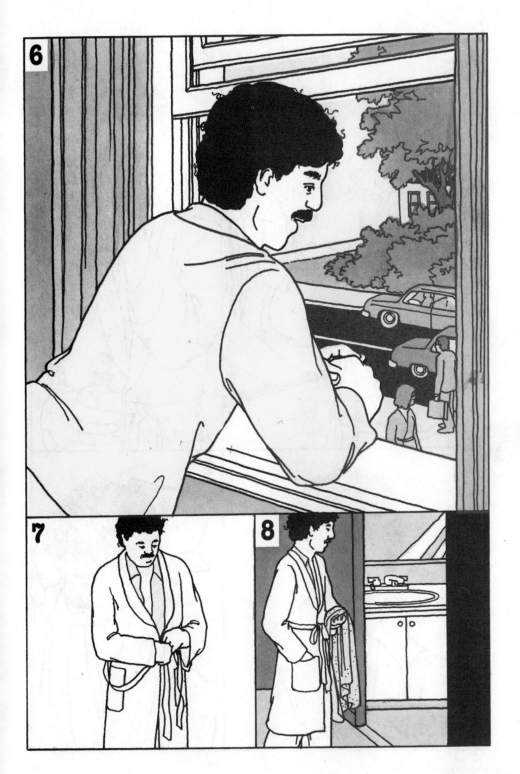

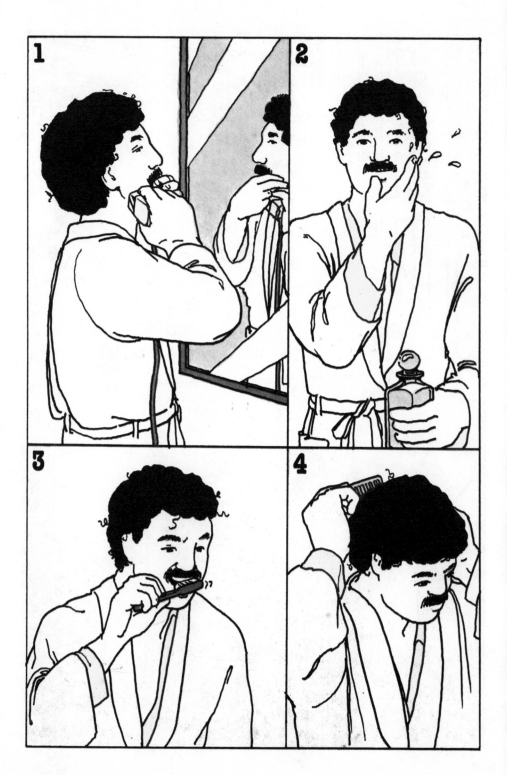

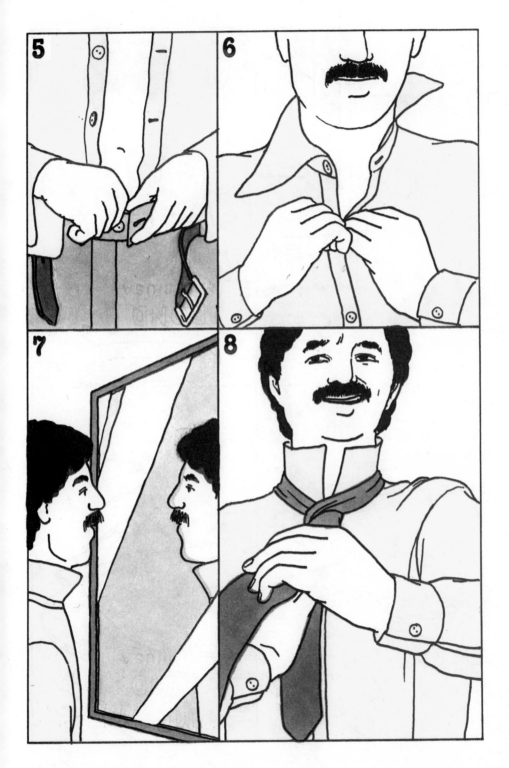

Sequence 1

1. Erik wakes up at seven o'clock.
2. He turns off the alarm clock.
3. He turns on the radio.
4. He listens to the news.
5. He gets out of bed.
6. He looks out the window.
7. He puts on his bathrobe.
8. He walks to the bathroom.

Sequence 2

1. He shaves with an electric razor.
2. He puts on after-shave lotion.
3. He brushes his teeth.
4. He combs his hair.
5. He puts on his pants.
6. He buttons his shirt.
7. He stands in front of the mirror.
8. He ties his tie.

Sequence 3

1. He goes into the kitchen.
2. He sits down at the table.
3. He butters his toast.
4. He puts salt on his eggs.
5. He pours cream in his coffee.
6. He puts sugar in it.
7. He picks up a spoon.
8. He stirs his coffee.

Sequence 4

1. He gathers his papers together.
2. He opens his briefcase.
3. He puts the papers inside.
4. He closes his briefcase.
5. He puts on his jacket.
6. He straightens his tie.
7. He picks up his briefcase.
8. He walks out the door.

Practice 1

Change *Erik* to *I*.
Example:
1. Erik wakes up at seven o'clock.
I wake up at seven o'clock.

Practice 2

End each sentence with *every morning*.
Example:
1. I shave with an electric razor.
I shave with an electric razor every morning.
2. I put on after-shave lotion.
3. I brush my teeth.
4. I comb my hair.
5. I put on my pants.
6. I button my shirt.
7. I stand in front of the mirror.
8. I tie my tie.

Practice 3

Change each sentence to the negative.
Example:
1. I go into the kitchen every morning.
   I don't go into the kitchen every morning.
2. I sit down at the table every morning.
3. I butter my toast every morning.
4. I put salt on my eggs every morning.
5. I pour cream in my coffee every morning.
6. I put sugar in it every morning.
7. I pick up a spoon every morning.
8. I stir my coffee every morning.

Practice 4

Change each sentence to a question with *you*.
Example:
1. I don't gather my papers together every morning.
   Do you gather your papers together every morning?
2. I don't open my briefcase every morning.
3. I don't put the papers inside every morning.
4. I don't close my briefcase every morning.
5. I don't put on my jacket every morning.
6. I don't straighten my tie every morning.
7. I don't pick up my briefcase every morning.
8. I don't walk out the door every morning.

CONVERSATION

What do you do every morning?

What time do you get up?
What is the first thing you do?
Do you listen to the radio?
Do you eat breakfast?
What do you do after breakfast?

THE TRIP TO WORK

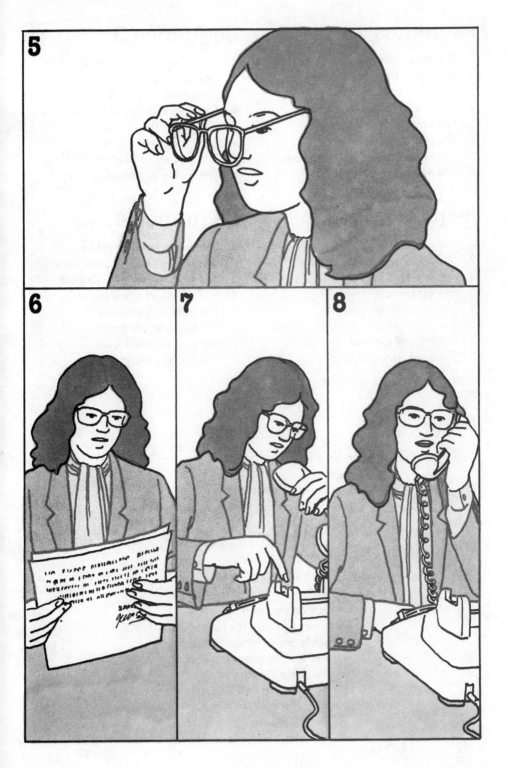

Sequence 1

1. Jessica walks down the street.
2. She enters the train station.
3. She buys a ticket.
4. She goes through the turnstile.
5. She runs to the platform.
6. She gets in line.
7. She takes out her handkerchief.
8. She wipes her forehead.

Sequence 2

1. She gets on the train.
2. She holds onto a strap.
3. She sees an empty seat.
4. She sits down.
5. She reads the newspaper.
6. She gives the conductor her ticket.
7. She gets off the train.
8. She heads toward the exit.

Sequence 3

1. She stands at the crosswalk.
2. She waits for the green light.
3. She crosses the street.
4. She goes into her office building.
5. She enters the elevator.
6. She pushes the button.
7. She gets off on the twelfth floor.
8. She walks down the hallway.

Sequence 4

1. She walks into her office.
2. She sets her briefcase on her desk.
3. She unlocks her desk drawer.
4. She takes out some papers.
5. She puts on her glasses.
6. She looks at the papers.
7. She makes phone calls.
8. She talks to a client.

Practice 1

End each sentence with *every day*.
Example:
1. Jessica walks down the street.
Jessica walks down the street every day.

Practice 2

Drop *every day* and add the adverb given.
Example:
1. She gets on the train. (always)
She always gets on the train.
2. She holds onto a strap. (sometimes)
3. She sees an empty seat. (sometimes)
4. She sits down. (sometimes)
5. She reads the newspaper. (sometimes)
6. She gives the conductor her ticket. (always)
7. She gets off the train. (always)
8. She heads toward the exit. (always)

Practice 3

Change each sentence to the negative.
Example:
1. She always stands at the crosswalk.
   She doesn't always stand at the crosswalk.
2. She always waits for the green light.
3. She always crosses the street.
4. She always goes into her office building.
5. She always enters the elevator.
6. She always pushes the button.
7. She always gets off on the twelfth floor.
8. She always walks down the hallway.

Practice 4

Remove *always* and end each sentence with *on Sundays*.
Example:
1. She doesn't always walk into her office.
   She doesn't walk into her office on Sundays.
2. She doesn't always set her briefcase on her desk.
3. She doesn't always unlock her desk drawer.
4. She doesn't always take out any papers.
5. She doesn't always put on her glasses.
6. She doesn't always look at the papers.
7. She doesn't always make phone calls.
8. She doesn't always talk to clients.

CONVERSATION

How do you get to work? to school?

Do you get there by train? by subway? by bus? by car?
How long does it take?
Do you usually read the newspaper?
Do you always go to work on Mondays?
Do you go to work on Sundays?

A BUSINESS LUNCH

Sequence 1

1. Erik and a businessman meet at ten o'clock.
2. They shake hands.
3. They take out their business cards.
4. They exchange cards.
5. They go into the salesroom.
6. They discuss the sales chart.
7. They look at sales reports.
8. They go out for lunch.

Sequence 2

1. They get on the elevator.
2. They get off on the main floor.
3. They leave the building.
4. They hail a taxi.
5. They get into the taxi.
6. They go to a restaurant.
7. They pay the taxi driver.
8. They get out of the taxi.

Sequence 3

1. They walk into the restaurant.
2. They find an empty table.
3. They sit down.
4. They order some drinks.
5. They make a toast.
6. They look at the menu.
7. They call the waiter.
8. They order lunch.

Sequence 4

1. They finish eating.
2. They get the bill.
3. They take out their wallets.
4. They leave a tip for the waiter.
5. They go to the cash register.
6. They give the cashier some money.
7. They get back their change.
8. They shake hands.

Practice 1

Change *Erik and a businessman* or *They* to *We*.
> Example:
> 1. Erik and a businessman meet at ten o'clock.
> *We meet at ten o'clock.*

Practice 2

Combine sentences 1 and 2, 3 and 4, 5 and 6, 7 and 8.
> Example:
> 1. We get on the elevator.
> 2. We get off on the main floor.
> *We get on the elevator and get off on the main floor.*
> 3. We leave the building.
> 4. We hail a taxi.
> 5. We get into the taxi.
> 6. We go to a restaurant.
> 7. We pay the taxi driver.
> 8. We get out of the taxi.

Practice 3

Insert *will* after *We*. Use the contracted form of the verb.

Example:

1 and 2. We walk into the restaurant and find an empty table.

We'll walk into the restaurant and find an empty table.

3 and 4. We sit down and order some drinks.

5 and 6. We make a toast and look at the menu.

7 and 8. We call the waiter and order lunch.

Practice 4

Shift *We'll* to the second part of the sentence, and start each sentence with *After*.

Example:

1 and 2. We'll finish eating and get the bill.

After we finish eating, we'll get the bill.

3 and 4. We'll take out our wallets and leave a tip for the waiter.

5 and 6. We'll go to the cash register and give the cashier some money.

7 and 8. We'll get back our change and shake hands.

CONVERSATION

Make plans for your next lunch or dinner in a restaurant.

How will you get there?
Who will you go with?
What will you eat?
Will you order drinks?
After you finish eating, what will you do?

AFTER WORK

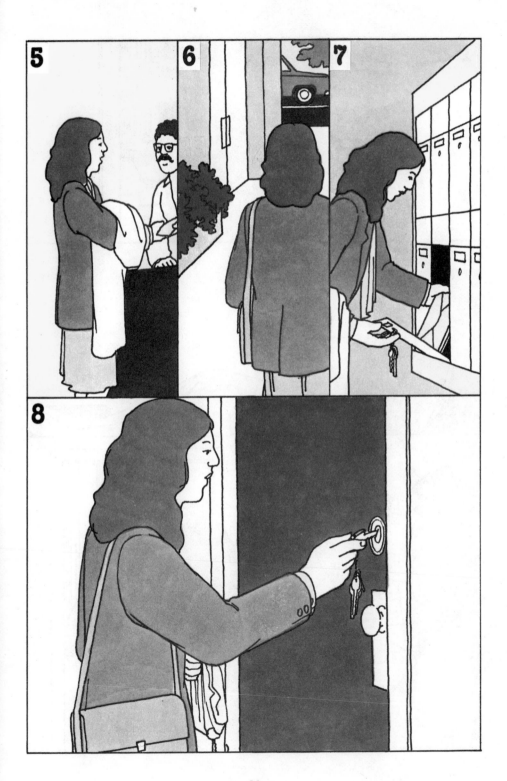

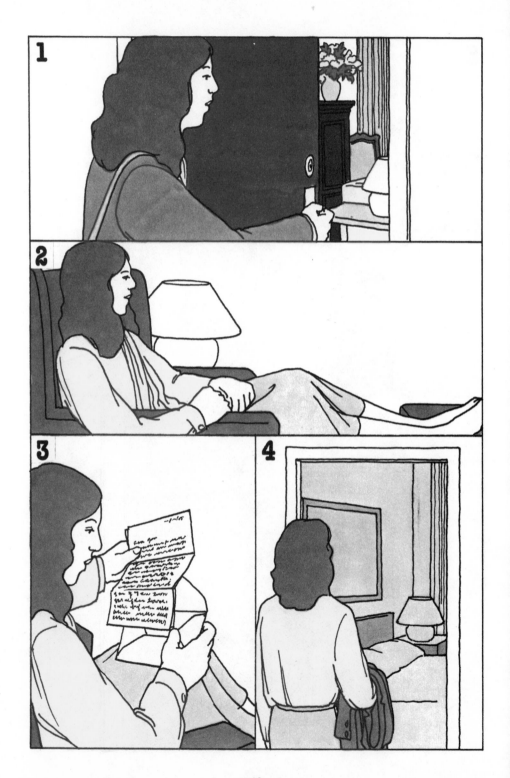

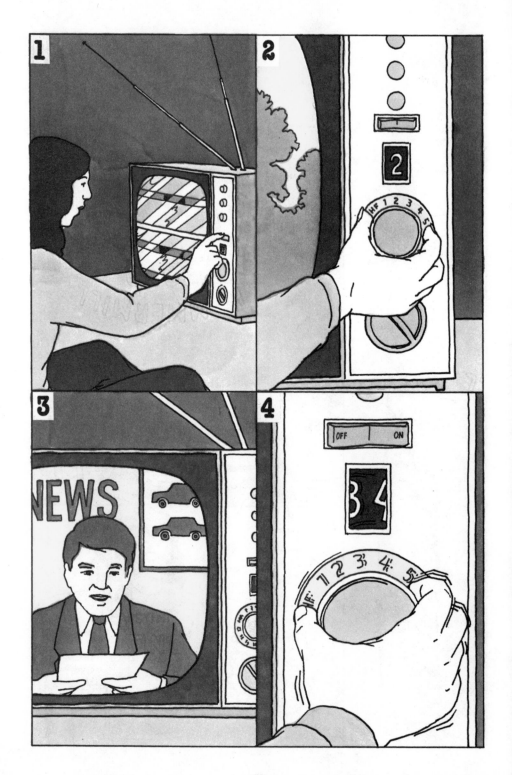

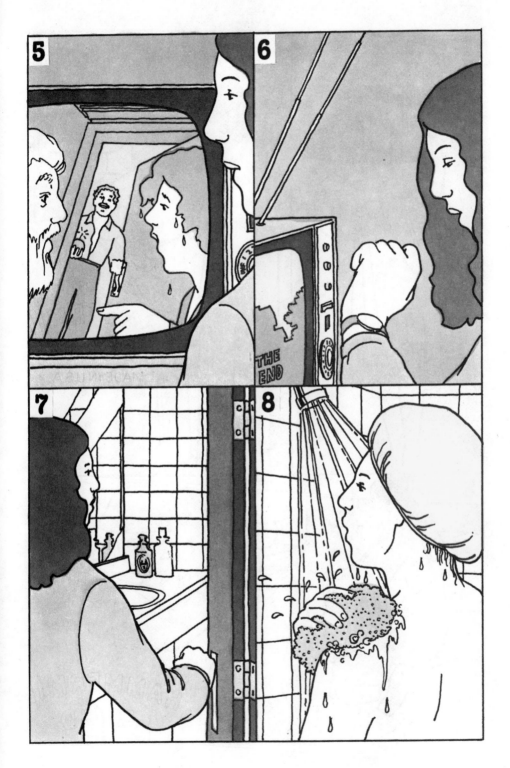

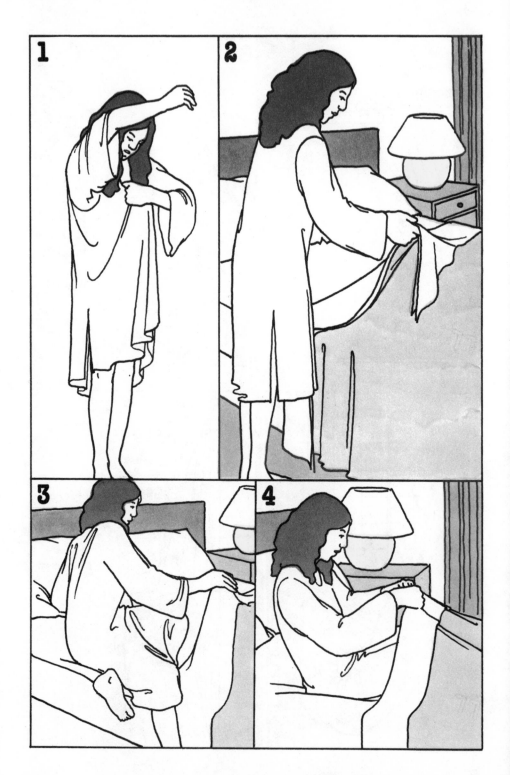

45

Sequence 1

1. She leaves the office at five o'clock.
2. She gets on the train.
3. She gets off at her stop.
4. She walks to the dry cleaners.
5. She picks up her dry cleaning.
6. She walks home.
7. She gets her mail.
8. She puts the key in the lock.

Sequence 2

1. She opens the door.
2. She relaxes in a chair.
3. She reads a letter.
4. She goes into the bedroom.
5. She changes her clothes.
6. She sets the table.
7. She puts some food on the table.
8. She has dinner.

Sequence 3

1. She turns on the television.
2. She turns to Channel Two.
3. She watches the news.
4. She changes the channel.
5. She finds a movie.
6. She looks at her watch.
7. She goes into the bathroom.
8. She takes a shower.

Sequence 4

1. She puts on her nightgown.
2. She turns back the covers.
3. She gets into bed.
4. She pulls up the covers.
5. She reaches over to the night table.
6. She sets her alarm clock.
7. She turns off the light.
8. She goes to sleep.

Practice 1

Insert *always* before the verb.
  Example:
  1. She leaves the office at five o'clock.
  She always leaves the office at five o'clock.

Practice 2

Begin each sentence with *When she gets home from work.*
  Example:
  1. She always opens the door.
  When she gets home from work, she always opens the door.
  2. She always relaxes in a chair.
  3. She always reads a letter.
  4. She always goes into the bedroom.
  5. She always changes her clothes.
  6. She always sets the table.
  7. She always puts some food on the table.
  8. She always has dinner.

Practice 3

Change *always* to *sometimes*.

Example:
1. When she gets home from work, she always turns on the television.
   When she gets home from work, she sometimes turns on the television.
2. When she gets home from work, she always turns to Channel Two.
3. When she gets home from work, she always watches the news.
4. When she gets home from work, she always changes the channel.
5. When she gets home from work, she always finds a movie.
6. When she gets home from work, she always looks at her watch.
7. When she gets home from work, she always goes into the bathroom.
8. When she gets home from work, she always takes a shower.

Practice 4

Ask questions with *when*.

Example:
1. She puts on her nightgown.
   When does she put on her nightgown?
2. She turns back the covers.
3. She gets into bed.
4. She pulls up the covers.
5. She reaches over to the night table.
6. She sets her alarm clock.
7. She turns off the light.
8. She goes to sleep.

CONVERSATION

What do you usually do in the evening?

Do you pick up anything on the way home?
When do you eat dinner?
Do you prefer to watch television or read at night?
If you watch television, what kind of programs do you like to watch?
When do you go to bed?

COIN-OPERATED
MACHINES

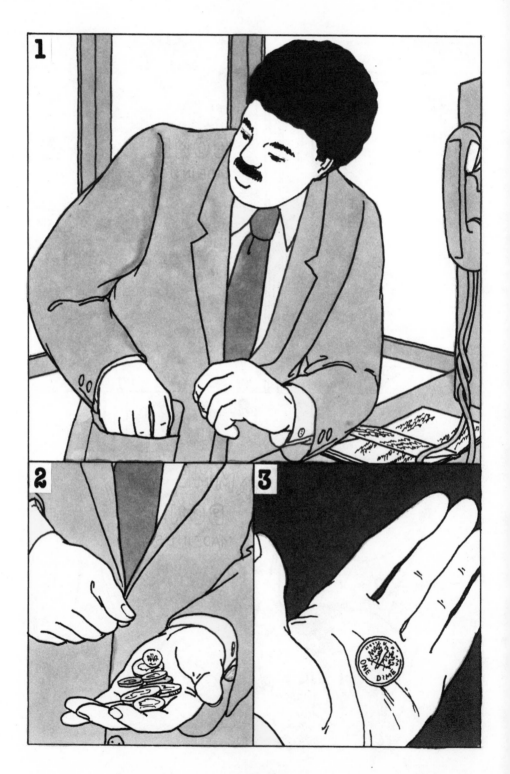

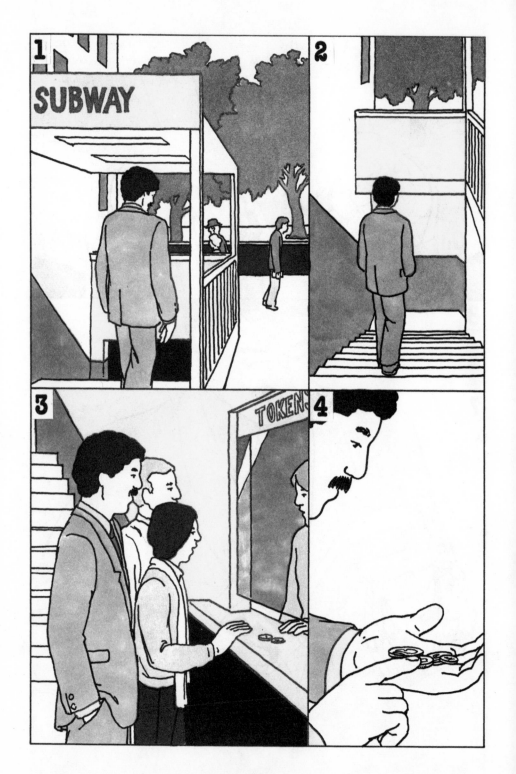

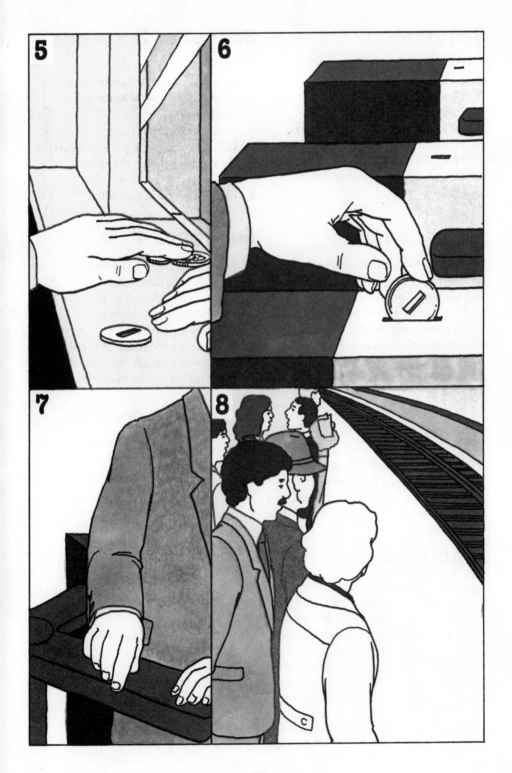

Sequence 1

1. He's walking to a phone booth.
2. He's pushing the door open.
3. He's stepping inside.
4. He's closing the door.
5. He's looking in the phone book.
6. He's looking for a number.
7. He's taking his notebook out.
8. He's writing the number down.

Sequence 2

1. He's reaching into his coat pocket.
2. He's looking at his change.
3. He's holding a dime.
4. He's picking up the phone.
5. He's dropping the coin in the slot.
6. He's dialing the number.
7. He's leaning against the glass.
8. He's hanging up the phone.

Sequence 3

1. He's walking along the street.
2. He's staring at the cigarette machine.
3. He's dropping some coins in the machine.
4. He's pressing a button.
5. He's picking up the pack of cigarettes.
6. He's picking up his change.
7. He's opening the pack.
8. He's taking out a cigarette.

Sequence 4

1. He's going into the subway.
2. He's walking down the steps.
3. He's going to the token booth.
4. He's taking out some coins.
5. He's buying a token.
6. He's putting the token in the slot.
7. He's going through the turnstile.
8. He's waiting on the platform.

Practice 1

Start each sentence with *Now*.
Example:
1. He's walking to a phone booth.
Now he's walking to a phone booth.

Practice 2

Drop *Now* and change *he's* to *I'm*.
Example:
1. Now he's reaching into his coat pocket.
I'm reaching into my coat pocket.
2. Now he's looking at his change.
3. Now he's holding a dime.
4. Now he's picking up the phone.
5. Now he's dropping the coin in the slot.
6. Now he's dialing the number.
7. Now he's leaning against the glass.
8. Now he's hanging up the phone.

Practice 3

Change each sentence to a question with *you*.
   Example:
   1. I'm walking along the street.
      Are you walking along the street?
   2. I'm staring at the cigarette machine.
   3. I'm dropping some coins in the machine.
   4. I'm pressing a button.
   5. I'm picking up the pack of cigarettes.
   6. I'm picking up my change.
   7. I'm opening the pack.
   8. I'm taking out a cigarette.

Practice 4

Change each sentence to a statement with *we*.
   Example:
   1. Are you going into the subway?
      We're going into the subway.
   2. Are you walking down the steps?
   3. Are you going into the token booth?
   4. Are you taking out some coins?
   5. Are you buying tokens?
   6. Are you putting the tokens in the slot?
   7. Are you going through the turnstile?
   8. Are you waiting on the platform?

CONVERSATION

How do you make a phone call?

How much does it cost?
Where do you look up the number?
What number can you dial for information?
Where do you drop the coin?
What do you do when you finish the phone call?

A VACATION TRIP

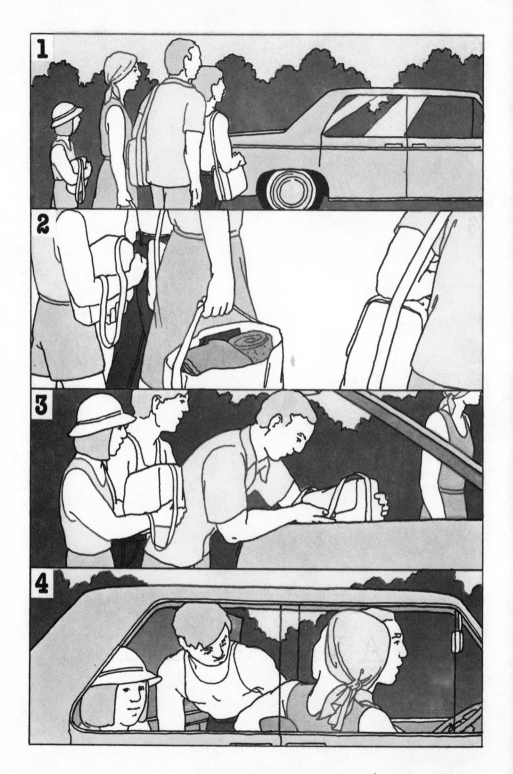

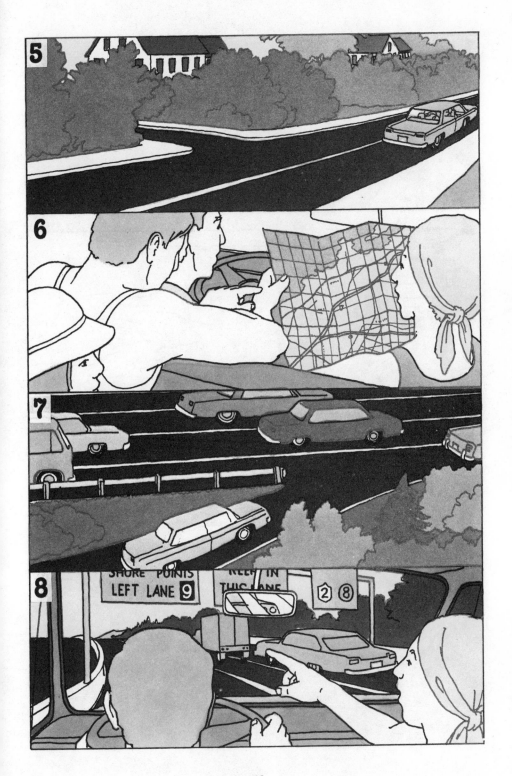

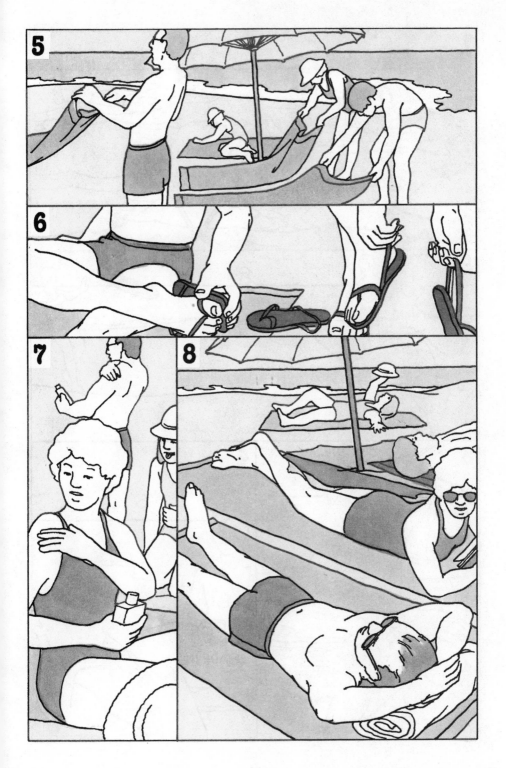

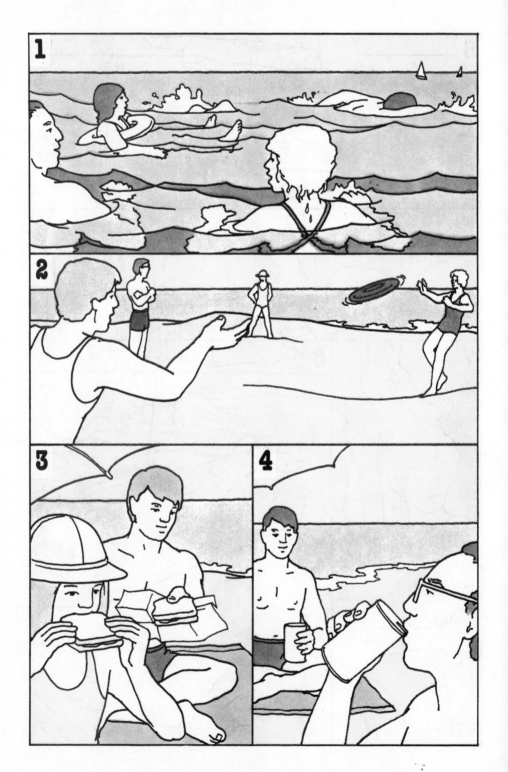

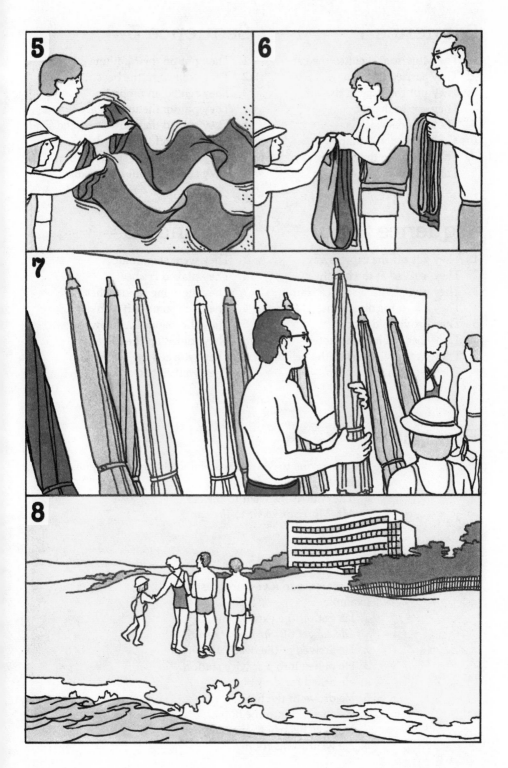

Sequence 1

1. The Morrisons went to the car.
2. They carried their bags.
3. They put the bags in the car.
4. They got in the car.
5. They drove away.
6. They looked at a map.
7. They got onto the expressway.
8. They followed the signs.

Sequence 2

1. They got off the expressway.
2. They arrived at the beach.
3. They pulled into a service station.
4. They asked for directions.
5. They drove to the hotel.
6. They checked into the hotel.
7. They gave their bags to the bellhop.
8. They went to their room.

Sequence 3

1. They put on their bathing suits.
2. They walked to the beach.
3. They rented an umbrella.
4. They put up the umbrella.
5. They spread their towels on the sand.
6. They took off their sandals.
7. They put on some suntan lotion.
8. They stretched out in the sun.

Sequence 4

1. They went swimming.
2. They played Frisbee.
3. They ate some sandwiches.
4. They had some soft drinks.
5. They shook out their towels.
6. They folded up the towels.
7. They returned the umbrella.
8. They walked back to the hotel.

Practice 1

Change *the Morrisons* to *Mr. Morrison* and change *they* to *he*.
Example:
1. The Morrisons went to the car.
   Mr. Morrison went to the car.

Practice 2

Change each sentence to a yes/no question.
Example:
1. He got off the expressway.
   Did he get off the expressway?
2. He arrived at the beach.
3. He pulled into a service station.
4. He asked for directions.
5. He drove to the hotel.
6. He checked into the hotel.
7. He gave his bag to the bellhop.
8. He went to his room.

Practice 3

Change each sentence to a negative statement and add *want to* before the verb.

Example:
1. Did he put on his bathing suit?
   He didn't want to put on his bathing suit.
2. Did he walk to the beach?
3. Did he rent an umbrella?
4. Did he put up the umbrella?
5. Did he spread his towel on the sand?
6. Did he take off his sandals?
7. Did he put on some suntan lotion?
8. Did he stretch out in the sun?

Practice 4

Change each sentence to a question.

Example:
1. He didn't want to go swimming.
   Did he want to go swimming?
2. He didn't want to play Frisbee.
3. He didn't want to eat any sandwiches.
4. He didn't want to have a soft drink.
5. He didn't want to shake out his towel.
6. He didn't want to fold up the towel.
7. He didn't want to return the umbrella.
8. He didn't want to walk back to the hotel.

CONVERSATION

What did you do on your last vacation?

Where did you go?
Did you take a map?
Who did you go with?
How long did you stay?
What did you take with you?

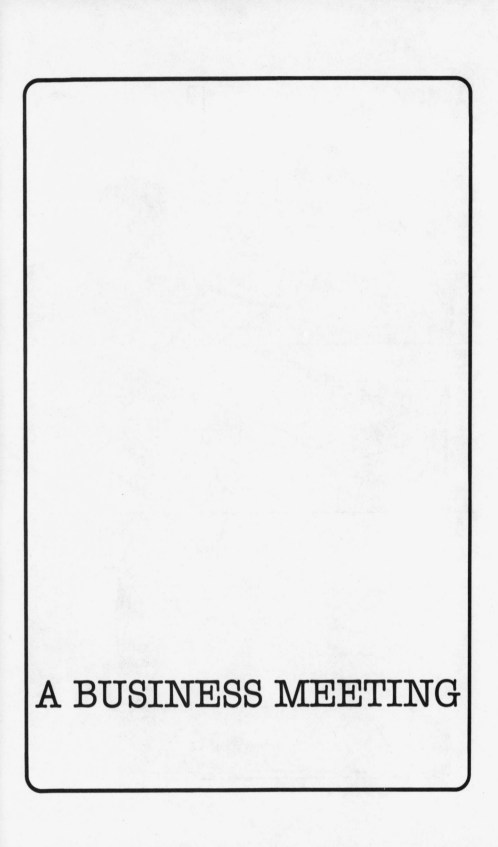

A BUSINESS MEETING

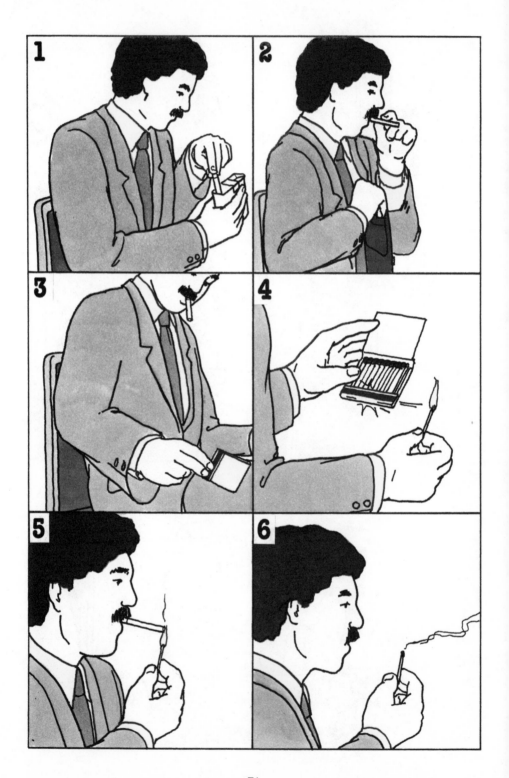

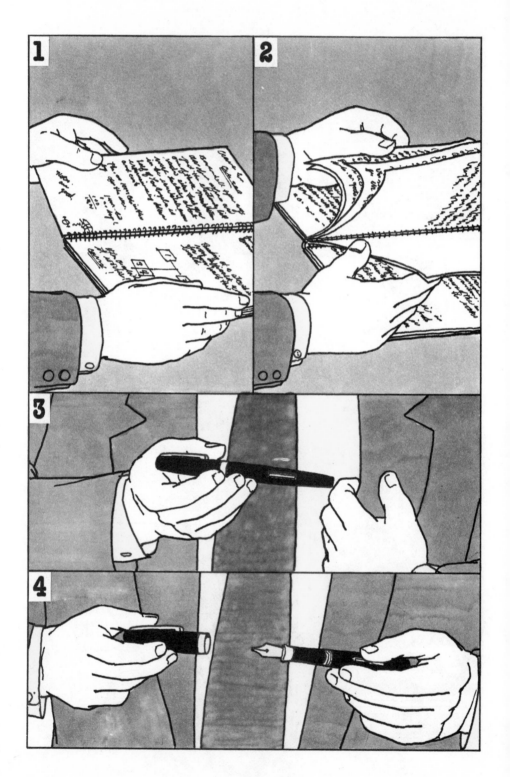

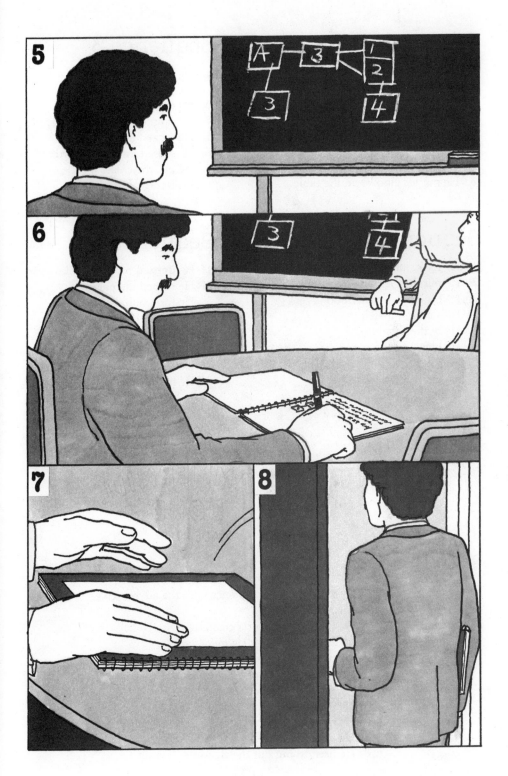

Sequence 1

1. Erik worked at his desk.
2. He looked at the clock.
3. He picked up his notebook.
4. He left his desk.
5. He walked through the office.
6. He went to the conference room.
7. He sat down at the table.
8. He put his elbows on the table.

Sequence 2

1. He took out a cigarette.
2. He put the cigarette in his mouth.
3. He took out a matchbook.
4. He struck a match.
5. He lit the cigarette.
6. He blew out the match.
7. He took a puff.
8. He put out the cigarette.

Sequence 3

1. He went to the blackboard.
2. He picked up a piece of chalk.
3. He drew a diagram.
4. He pointed to the diagram.
5. He picked up an eraser.
6. He erased the blackboard.
7. He put the eraser back.
8. He returned to his seat.

Sequence 4

1. He opened his notebook.
2. He turned the pages.
3. He took out his pen.
4. He took off the cap.
5. He looked at the blackboard.
6. He copied some notes.
7. He closed his notebook.
8. He left the room.

Practice 1

Tell the class what Erik *used to* do at his previous job.
Example:
1. Erik worked at his desk.
Erik used to work at his desk.

Practice 2

Drop *used to* and begin each sentence with the adverb given.
Example:
1. He used to take out a cigarette. (First)
First, he took out a cigarette.
2. He used to put the cigarette in his mouth. (Second)
3. He used to take out a matchbook. (Next)
4. He used to strike a match. (After that)
5. He used to light the cigarette. (Then)
6. He used to blow out the match. (After that)
7. He used to take a puff. (Then)
8. He used to put out the cigarette. (Finally)

Practice 3

Change each sentence to a yes/no question with *ever*.

Example:
1. First, he went to the blackboard.
   Did he ever go to the blackboard?
2. Second, he picked up a piece of chalk.
3. Next, he drew a diagram.
4. After that, he pointed to the diagram.
5. Then, he picked up an eraser.
6. After that, he erased the blackboard.
7. Then, he put the eraser back.
8. Finally, he returned to his seat.

Practice 4

Answer each question with the adverb given.

Example:
1. Did he ever open his notebook? (sometimes)
   He sometimes opened his notebook.
2. Did he ever turn the pages? (never)
3. Did he ever take out his pen? (sometimes)
4. Did he ever take off the cap? (never)
5. Did he ever look at the blackboard? (never)
6. Did he ever copy some notes? (never)
7. Did he ever close his notebook? (always)
8. Did he ever leave the room? (always)

CONVERSATION

Where do you work?

What do you do?
Where did you use to work?
What did you use to do at work?
Did you like the work you used to do?
Do you want to continue the work you're doing now?

A PARTY

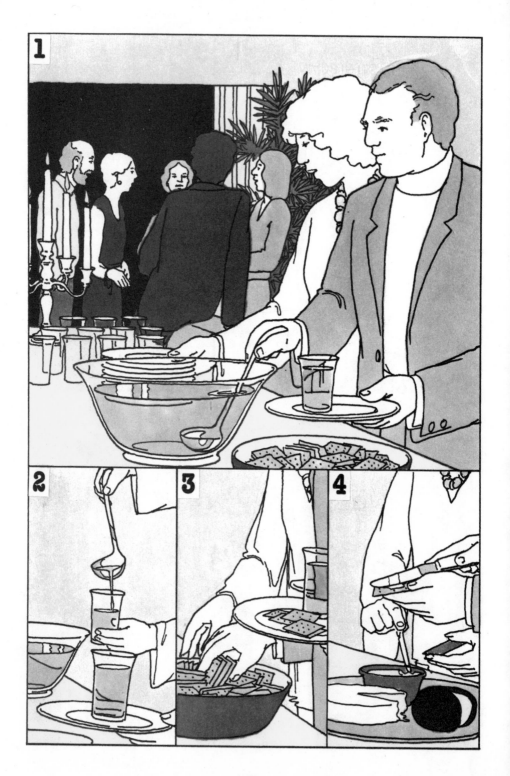

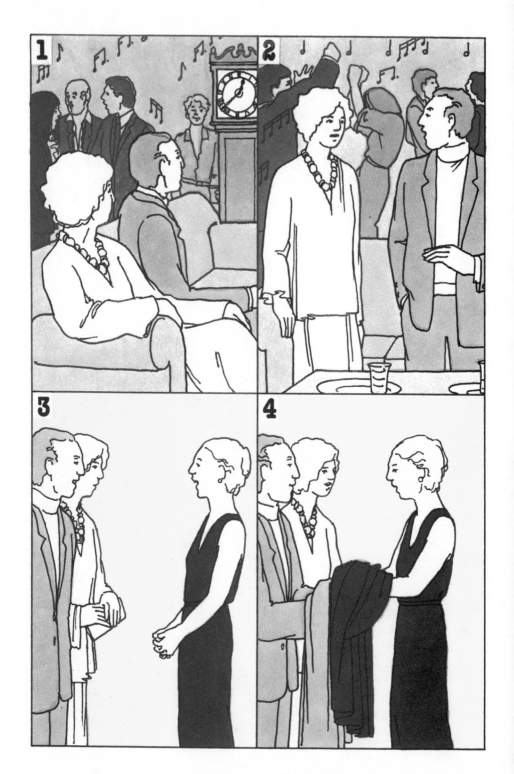

Sequence 1

1. Mr. and Mrs. Morrison checked the address.
2. They walked up the steps.
3. They entered the building.
4. They told the doorman their names.
5. They walked into the lobby.
6. They walked up one flight of stairs.
7. They looked at the name on the door.
8. They rang the bell.

Sequence 2

1. They said hello to the host.
2. They took off their coats.
3. They gave their coats to the hostess.
4. They saw a friend.
5. They went over to her.
6. They chatted for a few minutes.
7. They met the other guests.
8. They talked with them.

Sequence 3

1. They went to the punch bowl.
2. They filled their glasses.
3. They helped themselves to some crackers.
4. They put some cheese on the crackers.
5. They took some potato chips.
6. They sat down on a sofa.
7. They drank some punch.
8. They listened to music.

Sequence 4

1. They looked at the clock.
2. They got up off the sofa.
3. They walked over to the hostess.
4. They got their coats from her.
5. They put on their coats.
6. They said good-bye to the guests.
7. They thanked the host and hostess.
8. They left the party.

Practice 1

Combine sentences 1 and 2, 3 and 4, 5 and 6, 7 and 8. Begin with *After.*
Example:
1. Mr. and Mrs. Morrison checked the address.
2. They walked up the steps.
   After Mr. and Mrs. Morrison checked the address, they walked up the steps.

Practice 2

Combine sentences 1 and 2, 3 and 4, 5 and 6, 7 and 8. Change *After they* to *After saying.*
Example:
1 and 2. After they said hello to the host, they took off their coats.
   After saying hello to the host, they took off their coats.
3 and 4. After they gave their coats to the hostess, they saw a friend.
5 and 6. After they went over to her, they chatted for a few minutes.
7 and 8. After they met the other guests, they talked with them.

Practice 3

Combine sentences 1 and 2, 3 and 4, 5 and 6, 7 and 8. Begin each sentence with *During the party*.

Example:
1. They went to the punch bowl.
2. They filled their glasses.
   During the party, they went to the punch bowl and filled their glasses.
3. They helped themselves to some crackers.
4. They put some cheese on them.
5. They took some potato chips.
6. They sat down on the sofa.
7. They drank some punch.
8. They listened to music.

Practice 4

Combine sentences 1, 2, and 3; 4, 5, and 6; 7, 8, and your own. Follow the example.

Example:
1. They looked at the clock.
2. They got up off the sofa.
3. They walked over to the hostess.
   After looking at the clock, they got up off the sofa and walked over to the hostess.
4. They got their coats from her.
5. They put on their coats.
6. They said good-bye to the guests.
7. They thanked the host and hostess.
8. They left the party.

CONVERSATION

Describe the last party you went to.

What time did you get there?
What did you eat? drink?
Who was the host?
Did you meet anyone?
When did you leave?

A LETTER

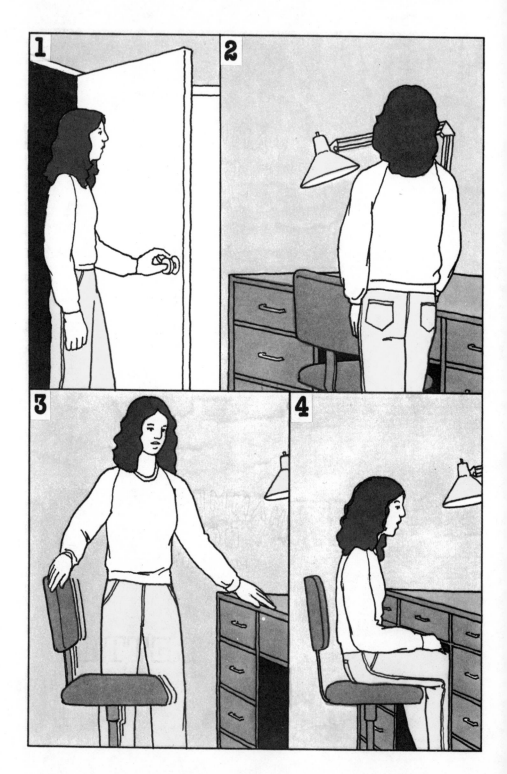

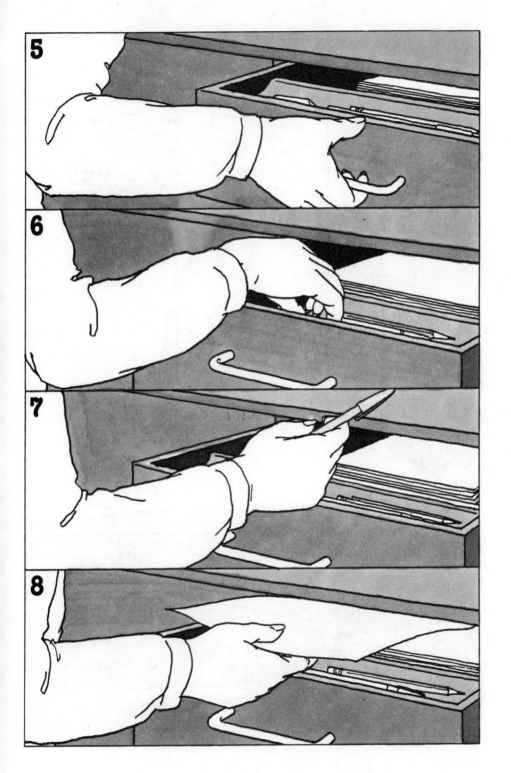

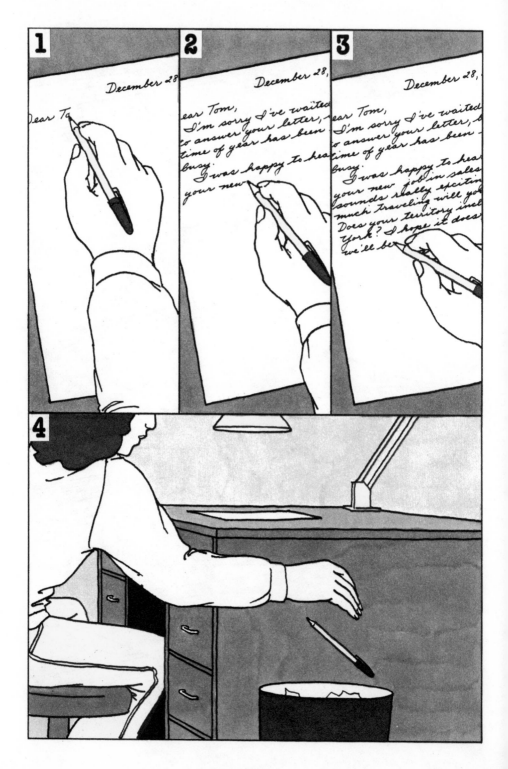

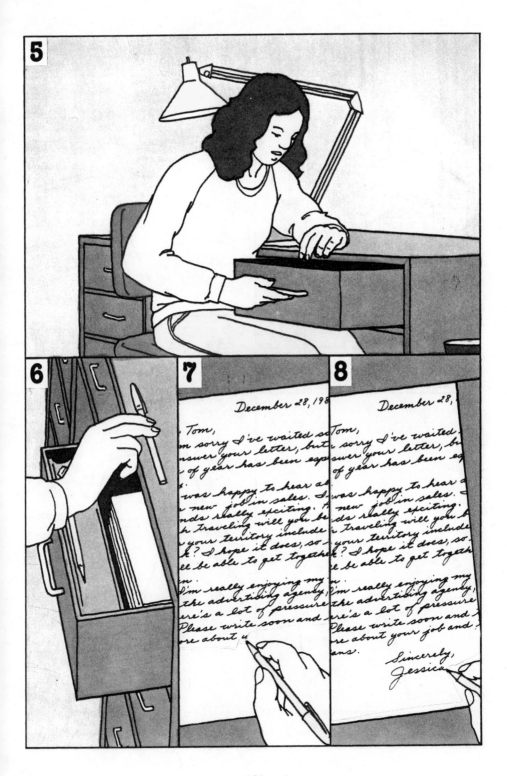

101

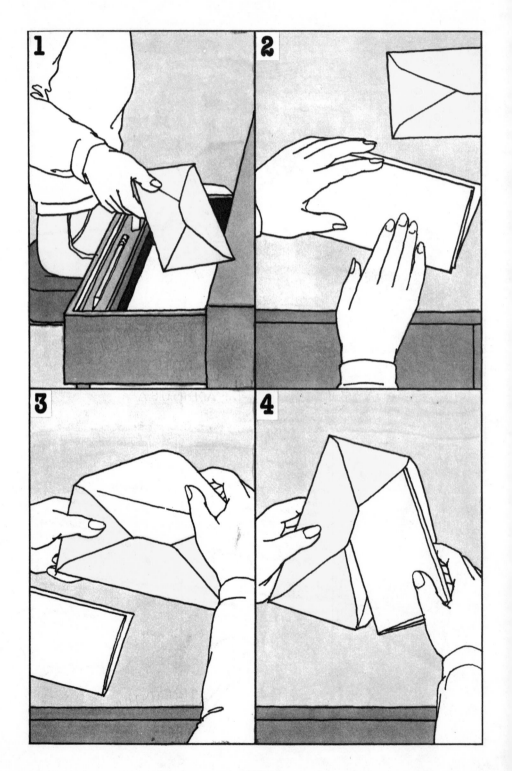

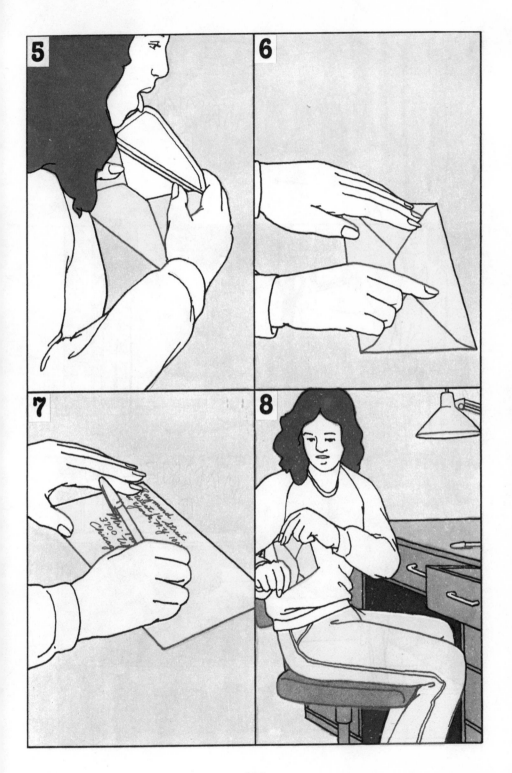

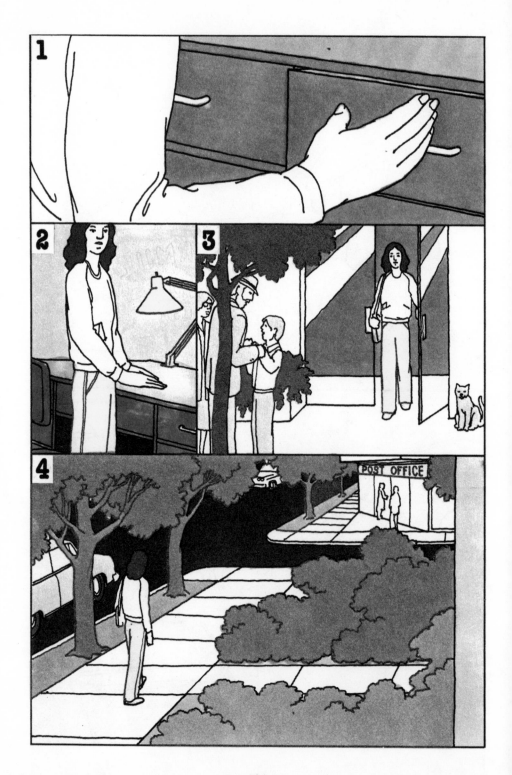

104

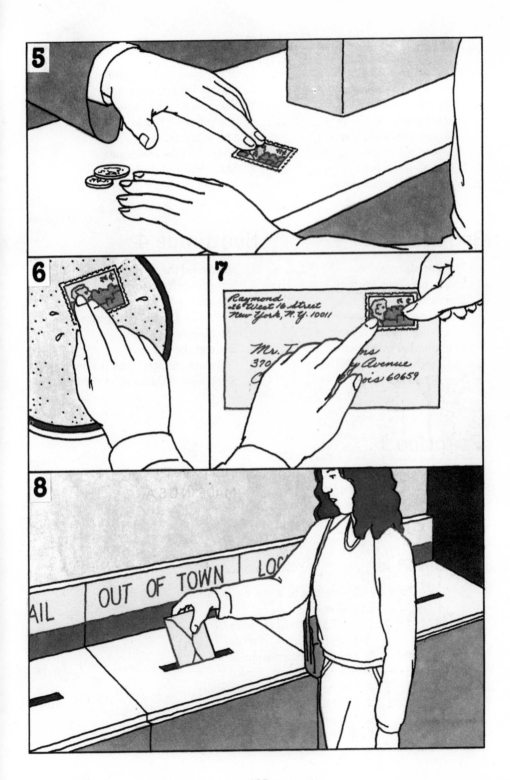

Sequence 1

1. Jessica walked into her room.
2. She walked over to her desk.
3. She pulled back the chair.
4. She sat down on the chair.
5. She opened the drawer.
6. She reached inside.
7. She took out a pen.
8. She took out some paper.

Sequence 2

1. She started to write.
2. She wrote some more.
3. She ran out of ink.
4. She threw the pen away.
5. She looked in the drawer.
6. She found another pen.
7. She finished writing the letter.
8. She signed her name.

Sequence 3

1. She took out an envelope.
2. She folded the letter.
3. She opened the envelope.
4. She put the letter in.
5. She licked the flap.
6. She sealed the envelope.
7. She addressed the envelope.
8. She put the letter in her pocket.

Sequence 4

1. She closed the drawer.
2. She got up from the desk.
3. She left the building.
4. She walked to the post office.
5. She bought a stamp.
6. She wet the stamp.
7. She stuck the stamp on the envelope.
8. She dropped the letter in the mailbox.

Practice 1

Change *walked* to *has walked*.
> Example:
> 1. Jessica walked into her room.
> *Jessica has walked into her room.*

Practice 2

Change each sentence to a yes/no question.
> Example:
> 1. She has started to write.
> *Has she started to write?*
> 2. She has written some more.
> 3. She has run out of ink.
> 4. She has thrown the pen away.
> 5. She has looked in the drawer.
> 6. She has found another pen.
> 7. She has finished writing the letter.
> 8. She has signed her name.

Practice 3

Change each sentence to a negative statement and end with *yet*.
Example:
1. Has she taken out an envelope?
   She hasn't taken out an envelope yet.
2. Has she folded the letter?
3. Has she opened the envelope?
4. Has she put the letter in?
5. Has she licked the flap?
6. Has she sealed the envelope?
7. Has she addressed the envelope?
8. Has she put the letter in her pocket?

Practice 4

Change *She* to *I*.
Example:
1. She hasn't closed the drawer yet.
   I haven't closed the drawer yet.
2. She hasn't gotten up from the desk yet.
3. She hasn't left the building yet.
4. She hasn't walked to the post office yet.
5. She hasn't bought a stamp yet.
6. She hasn't wet the stamp yet.
7. She hasn't stuck the stamp on the envelope yet.
8. She hasn't dropped the letter in the mailbox yet.

CONVERSATION

Do you enjoy writing letters?

Have you written any letters lately?
How many letters have you received in the past week?
Have you bought any stamps recently?
Where do you buy your stamps?
Have you mailed the last letter you wrote yet?

A CLOTHING STORE

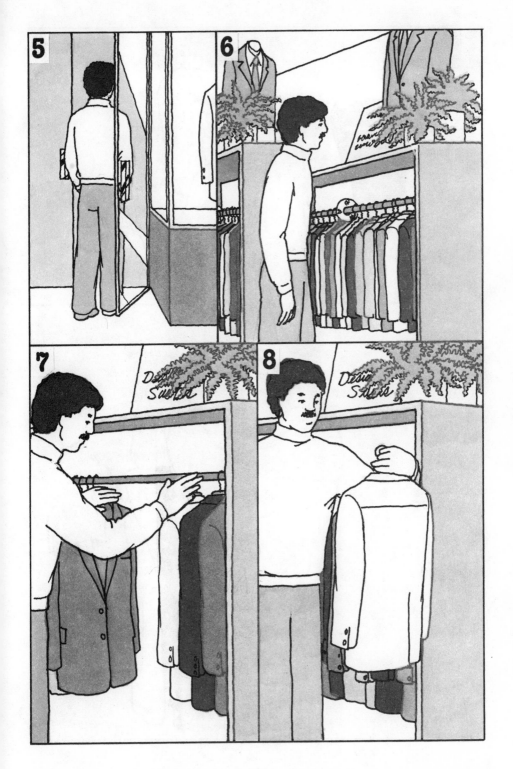

111

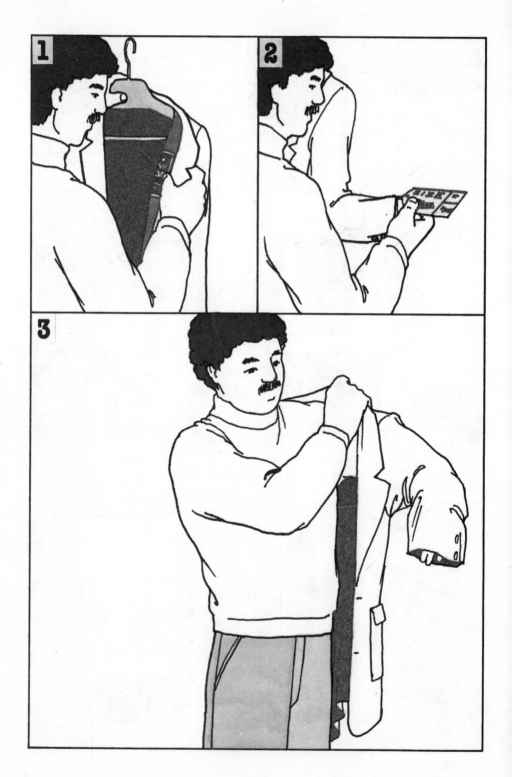

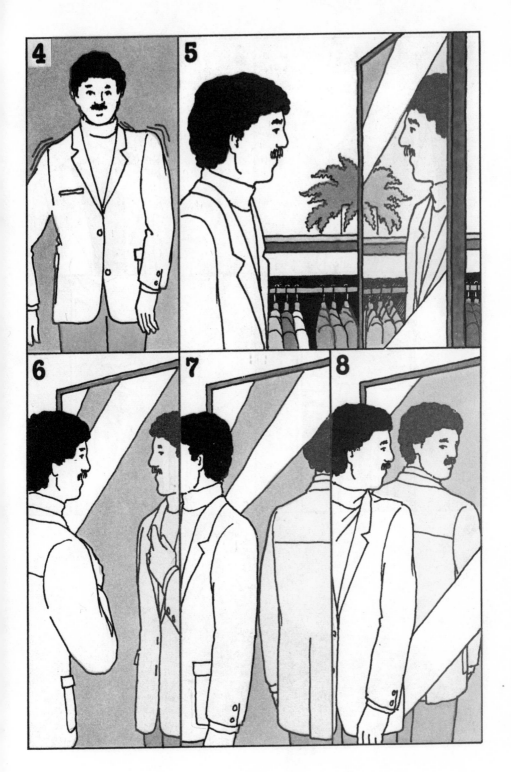

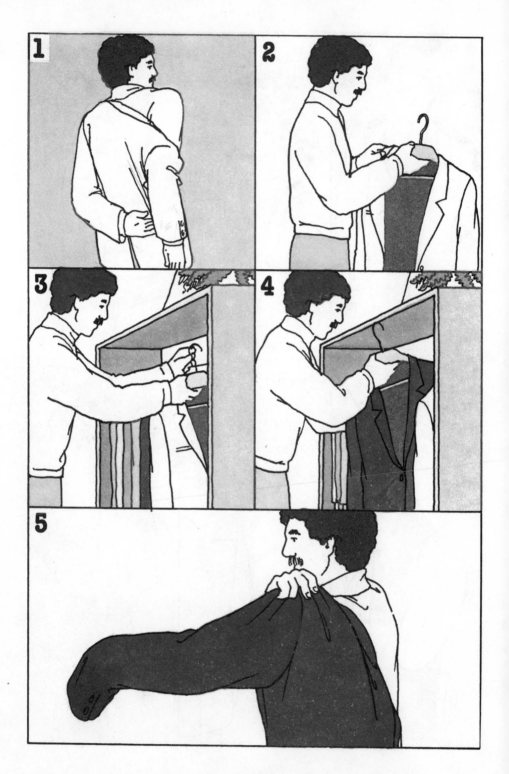

114

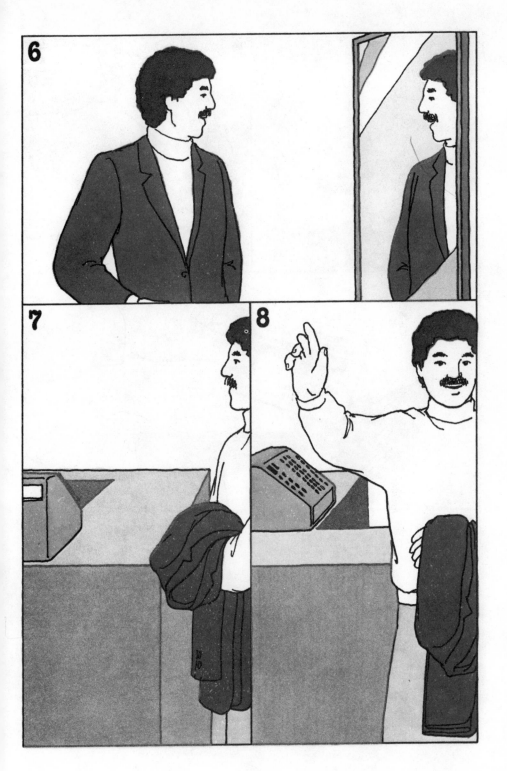

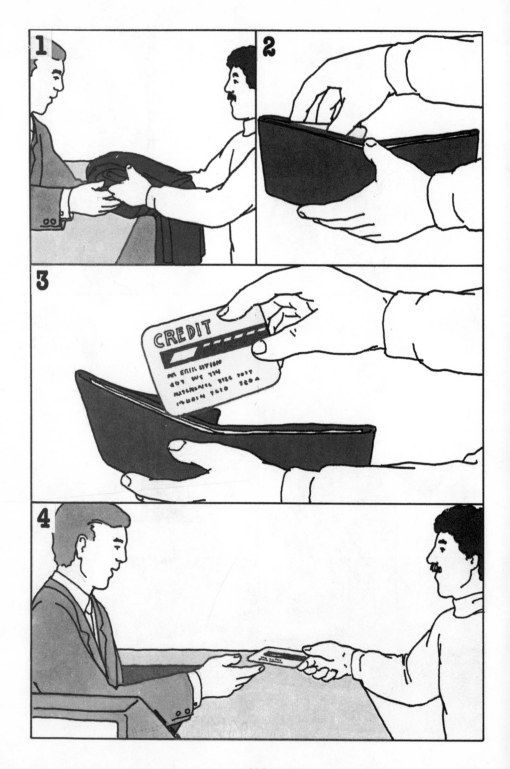

Sequence 1

1. Erik took a walk.
2. He stopped at a men's clothing store.
3. He looked in the window.
4. He looked at a sports jacket.
5. He went inside the store.
6. He went to the sports jacket section.
7. He reached for a sports jacket.
8. He took it off the rack.

Sequence 2

1. He looked at the label.
2. He checked the size.
3. He tried on the sports jacket.
4. He moved his shoulders.
5. He looked in the mirror.
6. He checked the front.
7. He turned around.
8. He checked the back.

Sequence 3

1. He took off the jacket.
2. He put it on a hanger.
3. He hung the jacket on the rack.
4. He found another one.
5. He put it on.
6. He checked the fit.
7. He took the jacket to the sales counter.
8. He called a clerk.

Sequence 4

1. He handed the jacket to the clerk.
2. He reached into his wallet.
3. He took out a credit card.
4. He handed the card to the clerk.
5. He signed his name.
6. He got a receipt.
7. He picked up the bag.
8. He walked out the door.

Practice 1

Add *decided to* before the verb.
Example:
1. Erik took a walk.
   Erik decided to take a walk.

Practice 2

Change *has to* to *had to*.
Example:
1. He has to look at the label.
   He had to look at the label.
2. He has to check the size.
3. He has to try on the sports jacket.
4. He has to move his shoulders.
5. He has to look in the mirror.
6. He has to check the front.
7. He has to turn around.
8. He has to check the back.

Practice 3

Change each sentence to a yes/no question.
Example:
1. He had to take off the jacket.
   Did he have to take off the jacket?
2. He had to put it on a hanger.
3. He had to hang the jacket on the rack.
4. He had to find another one.
5. He had to put it on.
6. He had to check the fit.
7. He had to take the jacket to the sales counter.
8. He had to call a clerk.

Practice 4

Change each sentence to a statement beginning with *He didn't want to* and ending with *but he had to.*
Example:
1. Did he have to hand the jacket to the clerk?
   He didn't want to hand the jacket to the clerk but he had to.
2. Did he have to reach into his wallet?
3. Did he have to take out a credit card?
4. Did he have to hand the card to the clerk?
5. Did he have to sign his name?
6. Did he have to get a receipt?
7. Did he have to pick up the bag?
8. Did he have to walk out the door?

CONVERSATION

When was the last time you went shopping for clothes?

What did you buy?
Were the clothes the right size or did they need alterations?
Did you try the clothes on before buying them?
How did you pay, with cash or with a credit card?
What do you enjoy or dislike most about shopping for clothes?

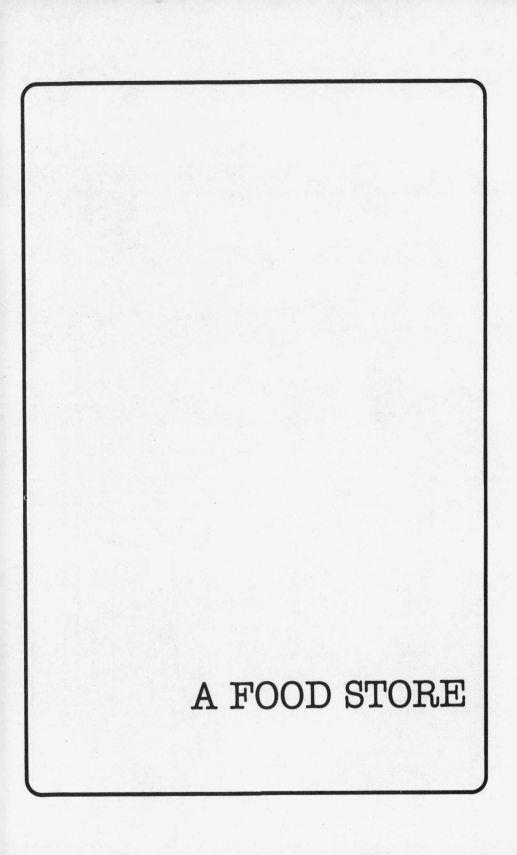

A FOOD STORE

122

Sequence 1

1. Drive into the parking lot.
2. Park the car.
3. Walk into the supermarket.
4. Go through the turnstile.
5. Get a shopping cart.
6. Check your grocery list.
7. Walk down the aisle.
8. Go to the meat section.

Sequence 2

1. Look at a steak.
2. Examine it carefully.
3. Look at the price.
4. Put it back.
5. Pick up a package of hamburger meat.
6. Check the price.
7. Take another package of hamburger meat.
8. Put the packages into the shopping cart.

Sequence 3

1. Stop at the produce section.
2. Pick out some tomatoes.
3. Have them weighed.
4. Select a head of lettuce.
5. Push the cart down the aisle.
6. Put some hamburger buns into the shopping cart.
7. Get some napkins.
8. Take a six-pack of soda.

Sequence 4

1. Go to the check-out counter.
2. Wait on line.
3. Put your groceries on the counter.
4. Watch the cashier ring up the bill.
5. Look at the receipt.
6. Pay the bill.
7. Pick up your shopping bags.
8. Carry them out of the store.

Practice 1

Start each sentence with *We'll*.
Example:
1. Drive into the parking lot.
   We'll drive into the parking lot.

Practice 2

Change *We'll* to *Let's*.
Example:
1. We'll look at a steak.
   Let's look at a steak.
2. We'll examine it carefully.
3. We'll look at the price.
4. We'll put it back.
5. We'll pick up a package of hamburger meat.
6. We'll check the price.
7. We'll take another package of hamburger meat.
8. We'll put the packages into the shopping cart.

Practice 3

Change *Let's stop* to *How about stopping.*

Example:
1. Let's stop at the produce section.
   How about stopping at the produce section?
2. Let's pick out some tomatoes.
3. Let's have them weighed.
4. Let's select a head of lettuce.
5. Let's push the cart down the aisle.
6. Let's put some hamburger buns in the shopping cart.
7. Let's get some napkins.
8. Let's take a six-pack of soda.

Practice 4

Change *How about going* to *We're going to go.*

Example:
1. How about going to the check-out counter?
   We're going to go to the check-out counter.
2. How about waiting on line?
3. How about putting your groceries on the counter?
4. How about watching the cashier ring up the bill?
5. How about looking at the receipt?
6. How about paying the bill?
7. How about picking up your shopping bags?
8. How about carrying them out of the store?

CONVERSATION

Plan your next food shopping trip.

What are you going to buy?
Are you going to a grocery store or a supermarket?
Which do you prefer and why?
Will you check the prices before making a purchase?
How will you get to the store?

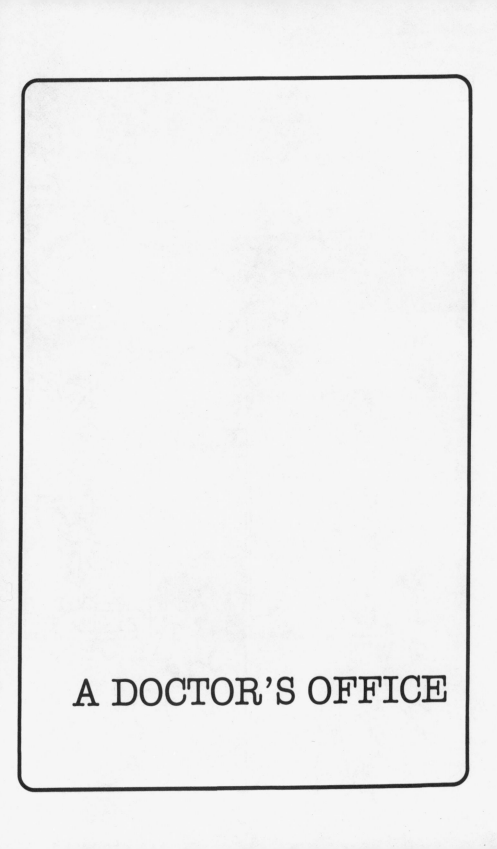

A DOCTOR'S OFFICE

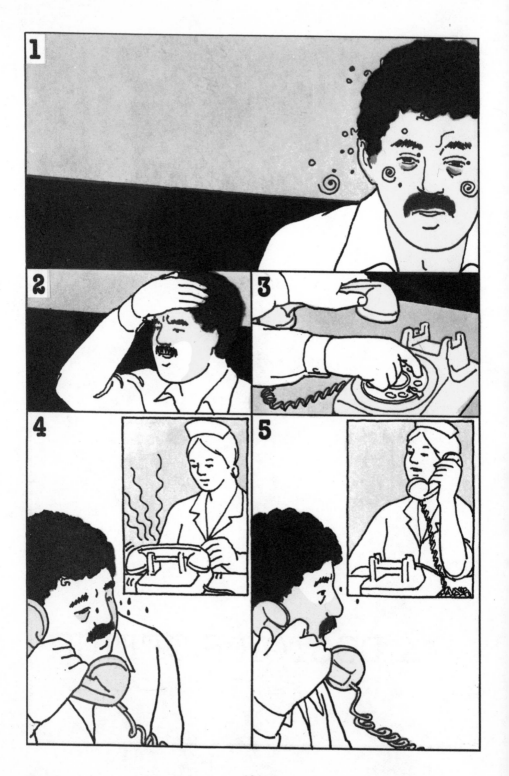

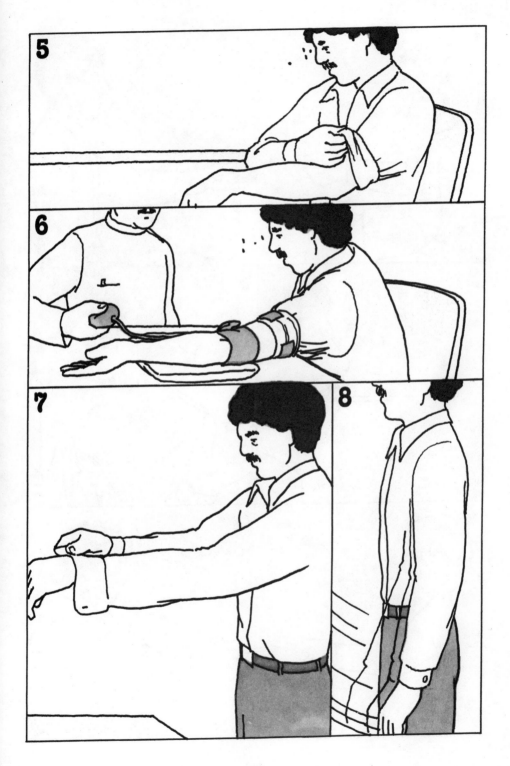

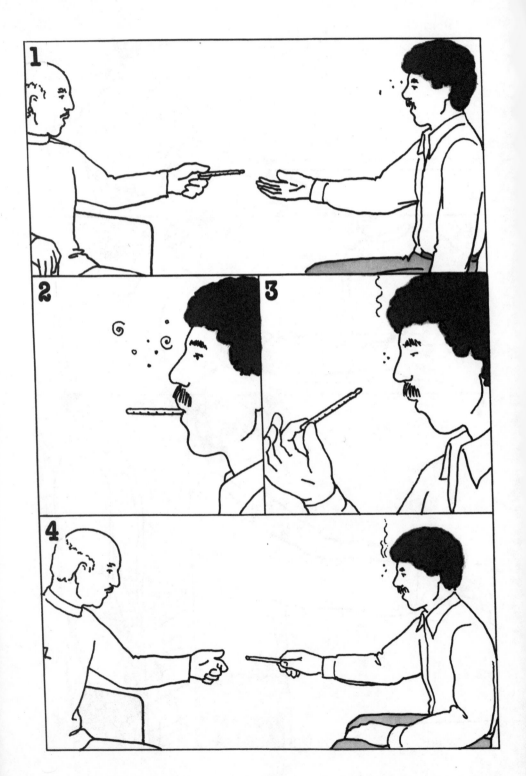

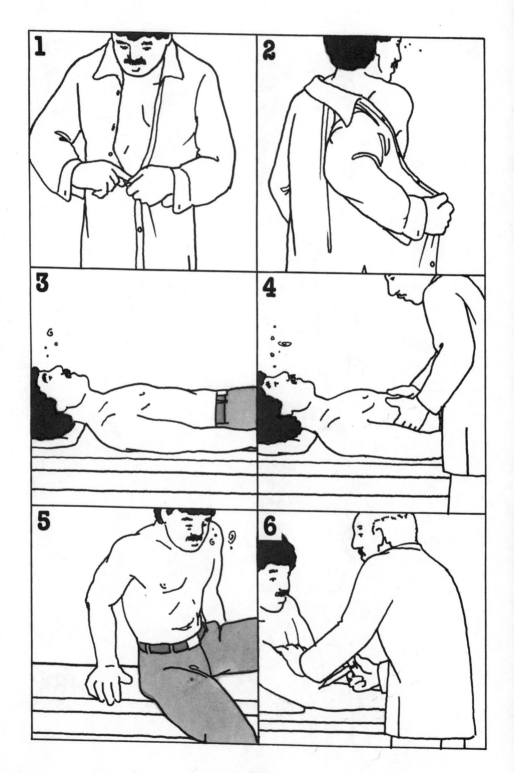

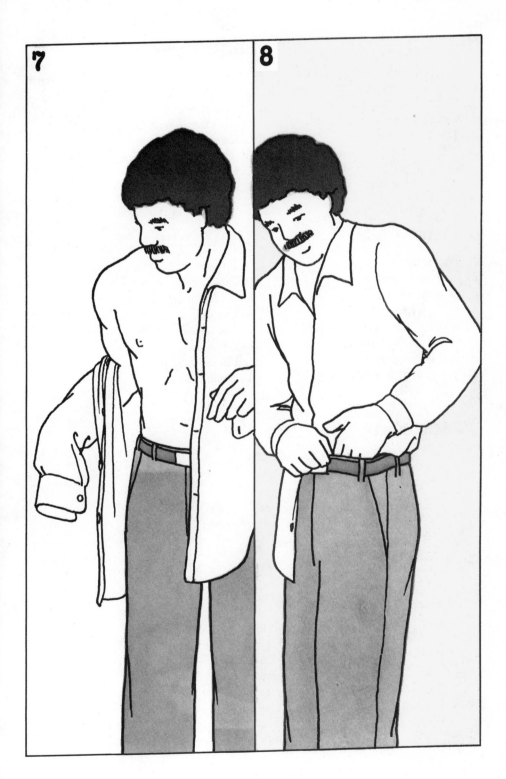

Sequence 1

1. Erik feels sick.
2. He has a headache.
3. Make a phone call.
4. Call the doctor's office.
5. Talk to a nurse.
6. Make an appointment.
7. Go to the doctor's office.
8. Walk up the steps.

Sequence 2

1. Wait in the waiting room.
2. Look at a magazine.
3. Go into the examination room.
4. Explain what's wrong.
5. Roll up your sleeve for a test.
6. Hold out your arm to the doctor.
7. Roll down your sleeve.
8. Put your arm down.

Sequence 3

1. Take the thermometer from the doctor.
2. Put it in your mouth.
3. Take it out.
4. Give it to the doctor.
5. Open your mouth.
6. Stick out your tongue.
7. Say, "A-a-ahh-h."
8. Close your mouth.

Sequence 4

1. Unbutton your shirt.
2. Take it off.
3. Lie down on the table.
4. Be examined by the doctor.
5. Get up off the table.
6. Get a shot.
7. Put on your shirt.
8. Tuck it in.

Practice 1

Begin each sentence with *He should*. Start with number 3 and omit number 8.

Example:
3. Make a phone call.
   He should make a phone call.

Practice 2

Change *He should* to *Please*.

Example:
1. He should wait in the waiting room.
   Please wait in the waiting room.
2. He should look at a magazine.
3. He should go into the examination room.
4. He should explain what's wrong.
5. He should roll up his sleeve for a test.
6. He should hold out his arm to the doctor.
7. He should roll down his sleeve.
8. He should put his arm down.

Practice 3

Change *Please* to *Could you* and combine sentences 1 and 2, 3 and 4, 5 and 6, 7 and 8.

Example:
1. Please take the thermometer from the doctor.
2. Please put it in your mouth.
   Could you take the thermometer from the doctor and put it in your mouth.
3. Please take it out.
4. Please give it to the doctor.
5. Please open your mouth.
6. Please stick out your tongue.
7. Please say, "A-a-ahh-h."
8. Please close your mouth.

Practice 4

Change *Could you* to *You can* and end each sentence with *now*.

Example:
1 and 2. Could you unbutton your shirt and take it off.
   You can unbutton your shirt and take it off now.
3 and 4. Could you lie down on the table and be examined by the doctor.
5 and 6. Could you get up off the table and get your shot.
7 and 8. Could you put on your shirt and tuck it in.

CONVERSATION

What should you do when you get sick?

Should you lie down?
Should you take your temperature?
Should you call a doctor?
Should you take medicine?
What medicine should you take?

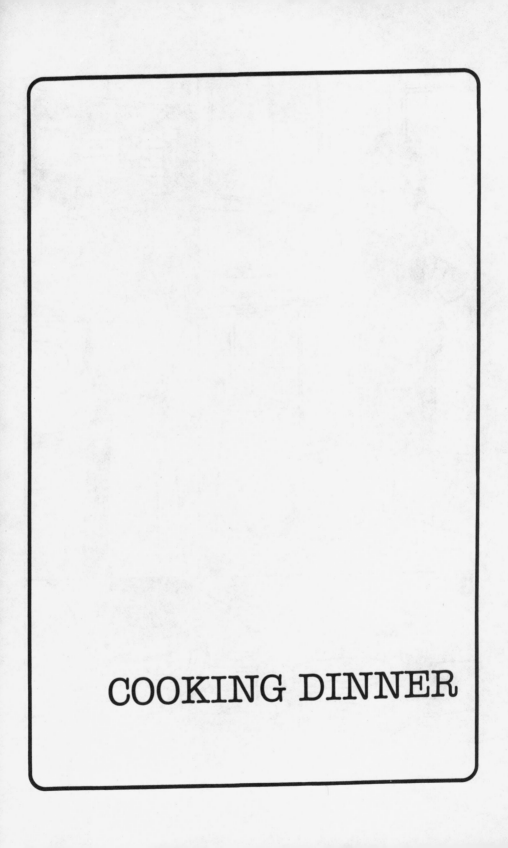

COOKING DINNER

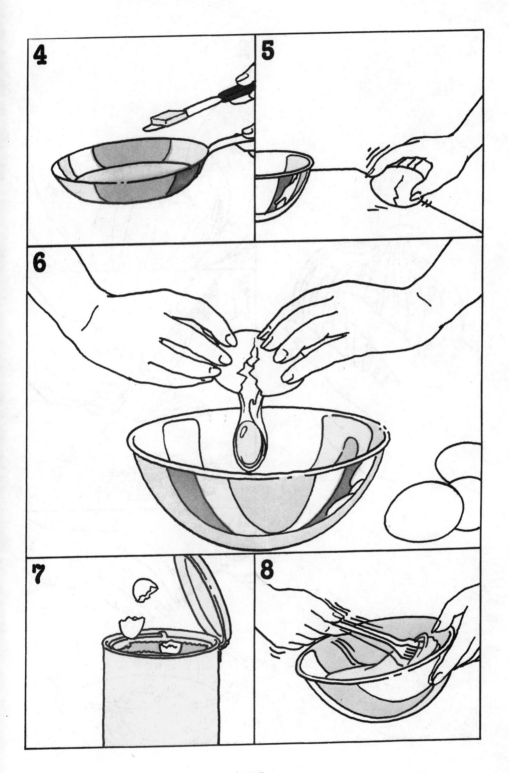

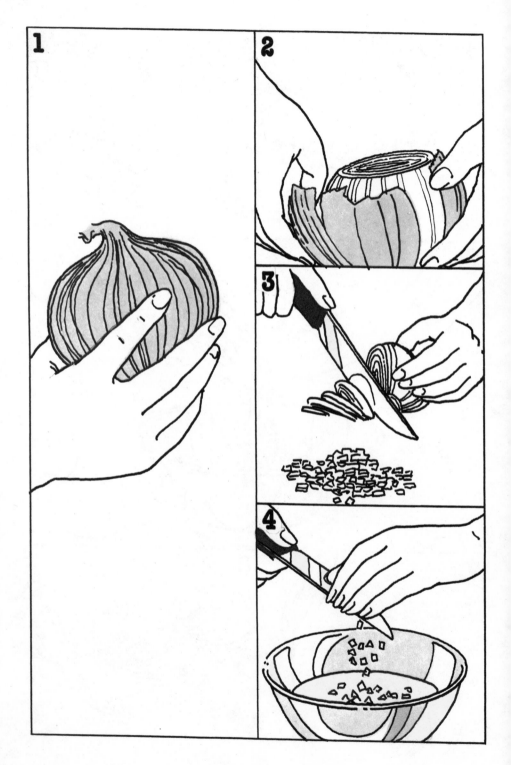

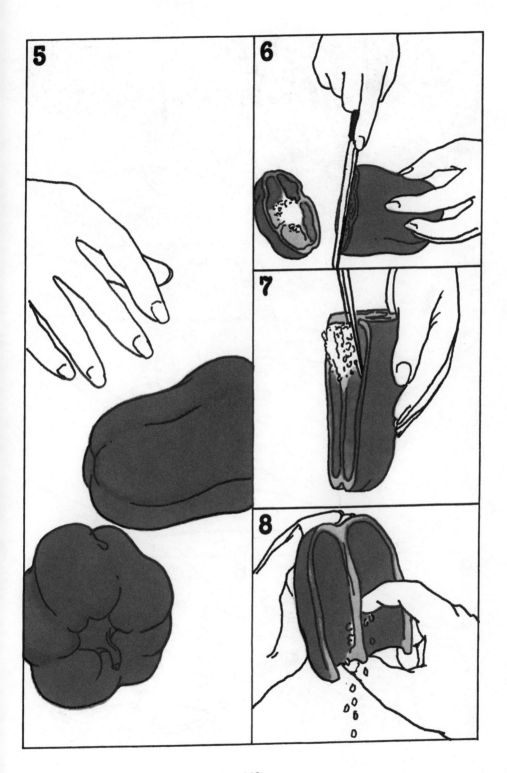

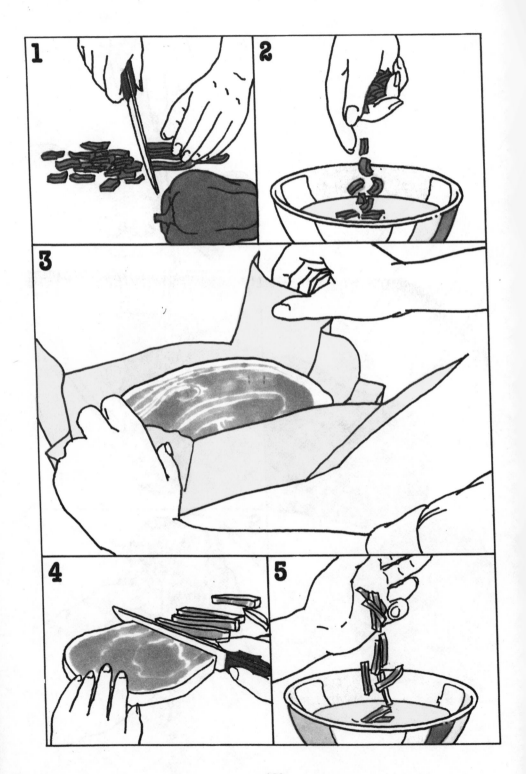

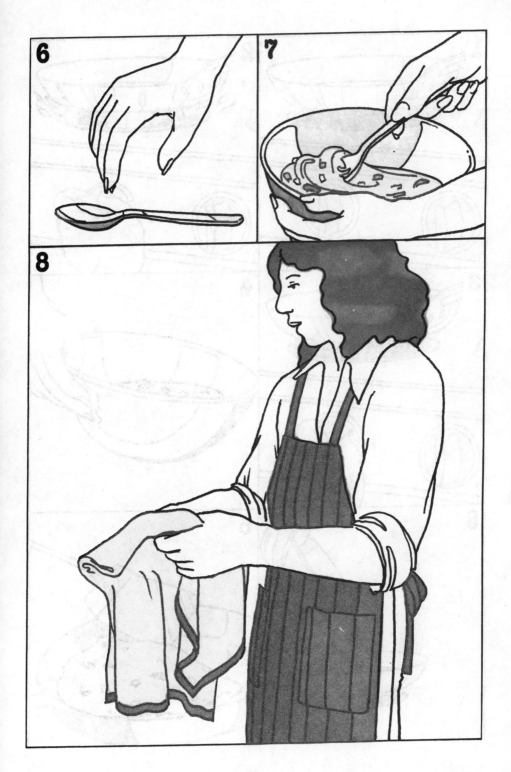

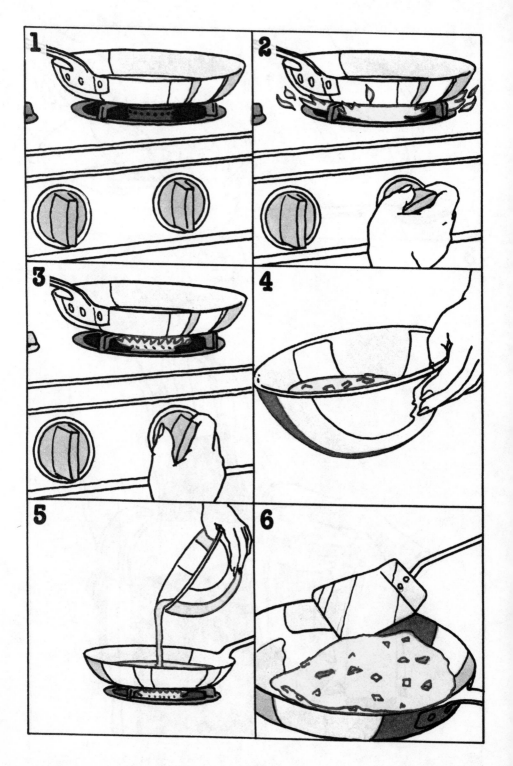

Sequence 1

1. Go to the kitchen.
2. Open the cupboard.
3. Put some things on the table.
4. Put some butter in a pan.
5. Tap an egg on the table.
6. Break the egg in a bowl.
7. Throw away the shell.
8. Beat the eggs.

Sequence 2

1. Pick up an onion.
2. Peel it.
3. Cut the onion into small pieces.
4. Add it to the eggs.
5. Reach for a green pepper.
6. Cut off the top.
7. Cut out the center.
8. Clean out the seeds.

Sequence 3

1. Chop up the pepper.
2. Put it in with the eggs.
3. Unwrap some ham.
4. Slice the ham into strips.
5. Drop the ham into the bowl.
6. Reach for a spoon.
7. Stir the eggs.
8. Wipe off your hands.

Sequence 4

1. Put the pan on the stove.
2. Turn on the gas.
3. Turn down the flame.
4. Pick up the bowl.
5. Pour the eggs into the pan.
6. Turn the eggs over.
7. Lift the eggs out of the pan.
8. Put the eggs on a plate.

Practice 1

Explain how to make an omelette. Begin each sentence with *You*.
Example:
1. Go to the kitchen.
   You go to the kitchen.

Practice 2

Add *should* after *You*.
Example:
1. You pick up an onion.
   You should pick up an onion.
2. You peel it.
3. You cut the onion into small pieces.
4. You add it to the eggs.
5. You reach for a green pepper.
6. You cut off the top.
7. You cut out the center.
8. You clean out the seeds.

Practice 3

Drop *You should* and begin each sentence with the adverb given.
Example:
1. You should chop up the pepper. (After that)
After that, chop up the pepper.
2. You should put it in with the eggs. (Next)
3. You should unwrap some ham. (Then)
4. You should slice the ham into strips. (After that)
5. You should drop the ham into the bowl. (Next)
6. You should reach for a spoon. (Then)
7. You should stir the eggs. (After that)
8. You should wipe off your hands. (Finally)

Practice 4

Change each adverb to *And then*.
Example:
1. After that, put the pan on the stove.
And then put the pan on the stove.
2. Next, turn on the gas.
3. Then, turn down the flame.
4. After that, pick up the bowl.
5. Next, pour the eggs into the pan.
6. Then, turn the eggs over.
7. After that, lift the eggs out of the pan.
8. Finally, put the eggs on a plate.

CONVERSATION

Describe one of your recipes.

What are you going to make?
What do you need?
Do you need a knife? a bowl? a pan? a spoon?
What do you do first?
And after that?

A FLAT TIRE

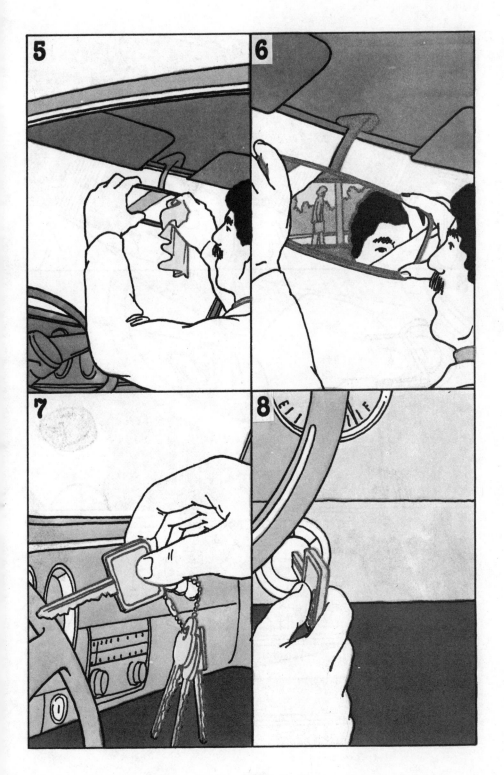

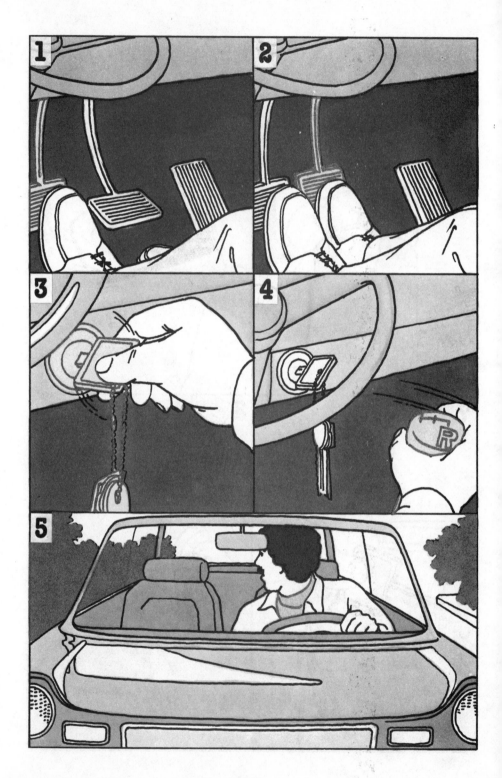

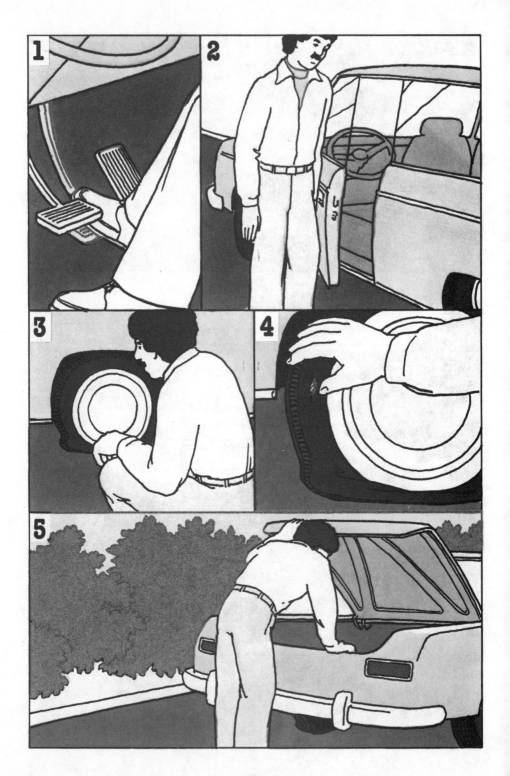

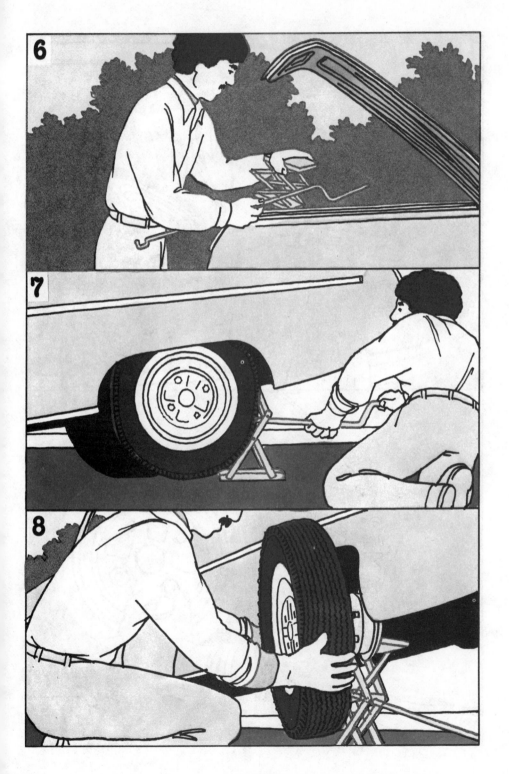

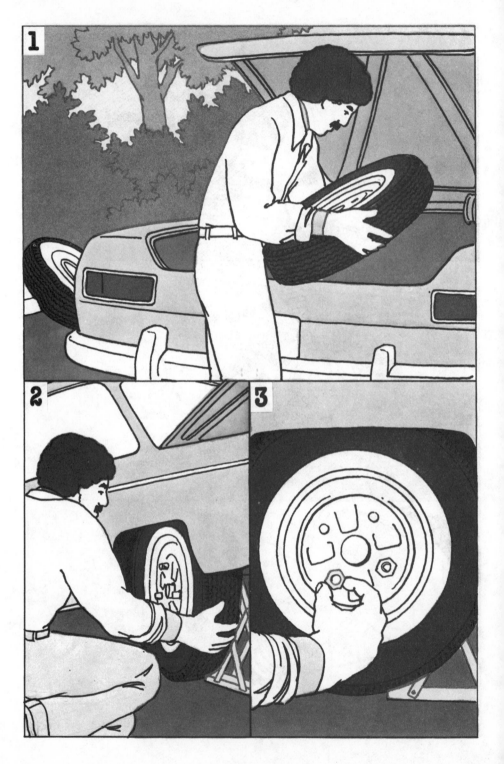

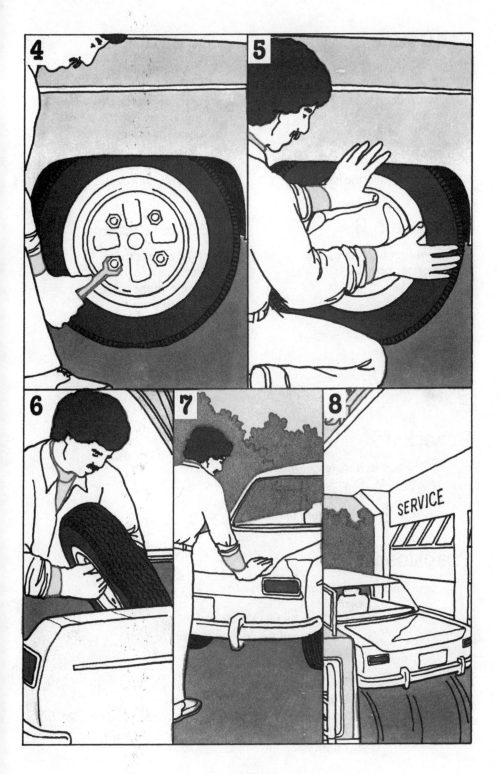

Sequence 1

1. Get into the car.
2. Move the seat back.
3. Shut the door.
4. Fasten the seat belt.
5. Clean the mirror.
6. Adjust it.
7. Take out your key.
8. Put the key into the ignition.

Sequence 2

1. Put your foot on the clutch.
2. Step on the brake.
3. Turn the key.
4. Shift into reverse.
5. Look behind you.
6. Release the clutch.
7. Step on the gas.
8. Back up.

Sequence 3

1. Step on the brake.
2. Get out of the car.
3. Examine the flat tire.
4. Find the hole in it.
5. Open the trunk.
6. Take out the jack.
7. Jack up the car.
8. Take off the wheel.

Sequence 4

1. Take out the spare.
2. Put it on.
3. Screw on the nuts.
4. Tighten them.
5. Put on the hubcap.
6. Put the flat tire in the trunk.
7. Close the trunk.
8. Drive to a service station.

Practice 1

Start each sentence with *I*.
Example:
1. Get into the car.
I get into the car.

Practice 2

Start each sentence with *I have to*.
Example:
1. I put my foot on the clutch.
I have to put my foot on the clutch.
2. I step on the brake.
3. I turn the key.
4. I shift into reverse.
5. I look behind me.
6. I release the clutch.
7. I step on the gas.
8. I back up.

Practice 3

Put *will* before *have to*. Use the contracted form.
Example:
1. I have to step on the brake.
   I'll have to step on the brake.
2. I have to get out of the car.
3. I have to examine the flat tire.
4. I have to find the hole in it.
5. I have to open the trunk.
6. I have to take out the jack.
7. I have to jack up the car.
8. I have to take off the wheel.

Practice 4

Change *will have to* to *am going to*. Use the contracted form.
Example:
1. I'll have to take out the spare.
   I'm going to take out the spare.
2. I'll have to put it on.
3. I'll have to screw on the nuts.
4. I'll have to tighten them.
5. I'll have to put on the hubcap.
6. I'll have to put the flat tire in the trunk.
7. I'll have to close the trunk.
8. I'll have to drive to a service station.

CONVERSATION

What do you have to do when you get a flat tire?

When you get a flat tire, do you fix it or does someone else?
Should you always carry a spare tire in the trunk of your car?
Do you have to use a jack to lift the car?
Do you have to take off the wheel?
After putting on the spare tire, why is it important to go to a service station?

HOUSE CLEANING

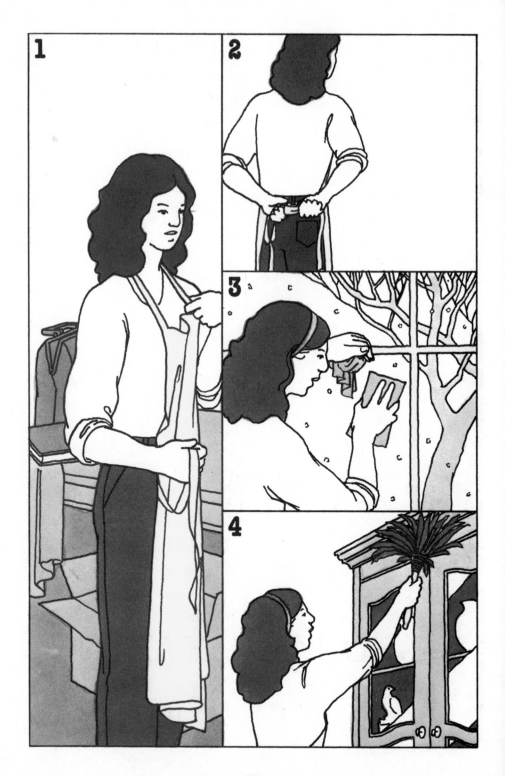

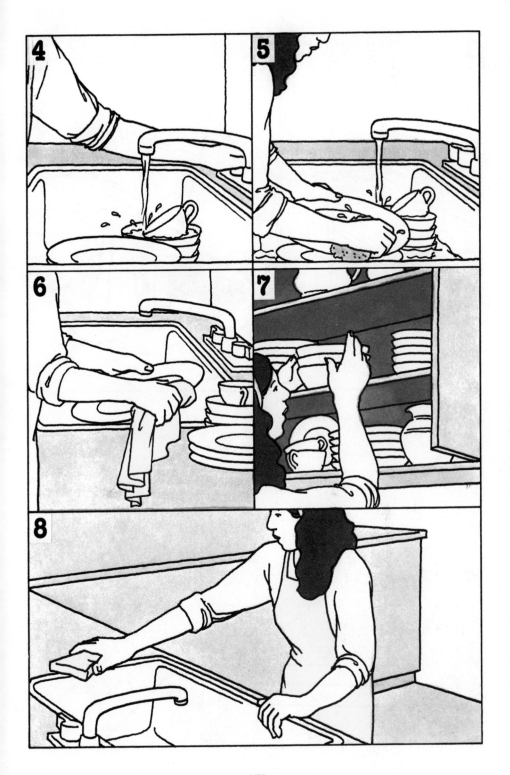

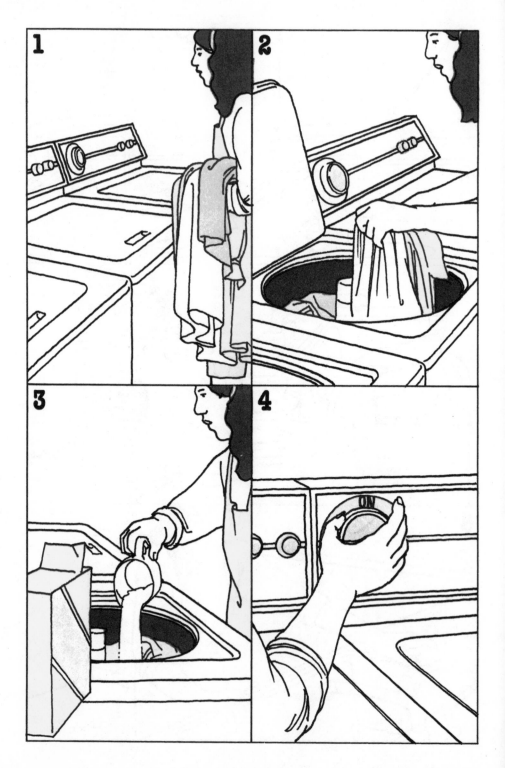

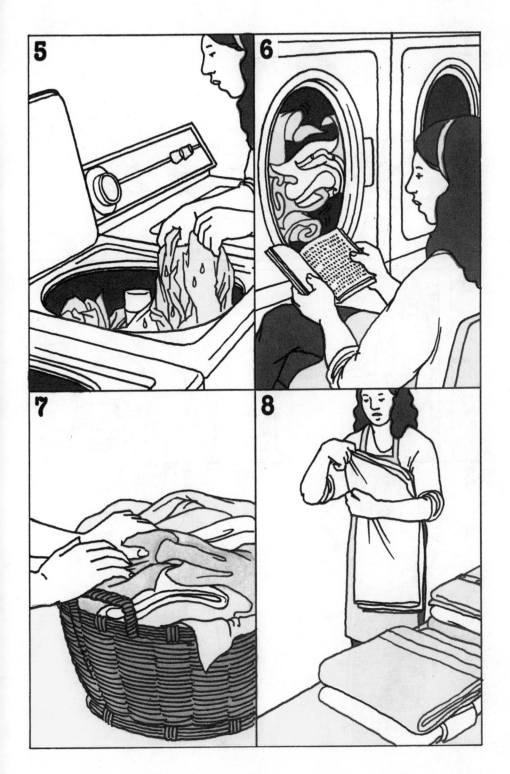

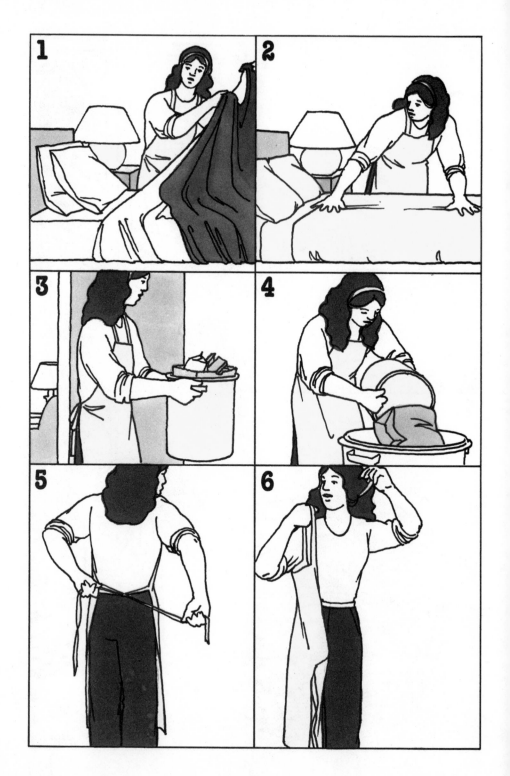

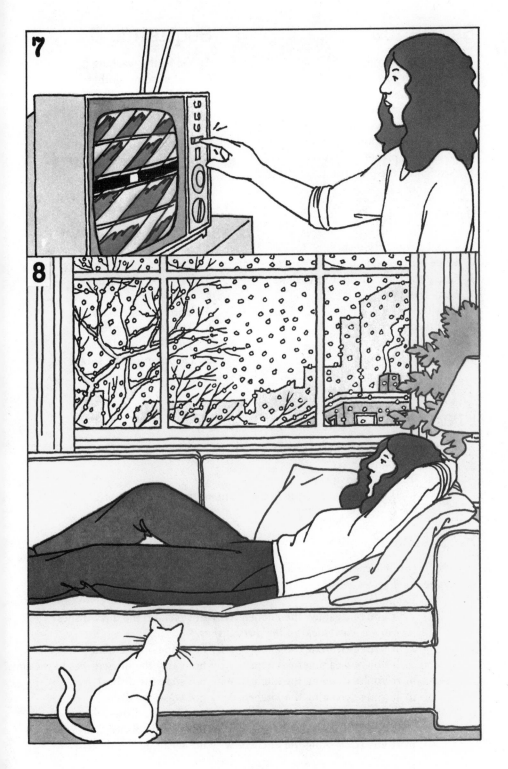

Sequence 1

1. Put on an apron.
2. Tie the strings.
3. Wash the windows.
4. Dust the furniture.
5. Plug in the vacuum cleaner.
6. Vacuum the floor.
7. Water the plants.
8. Straighten the pictures.

Sequence 2

1. Pick up the dirty dishes.
2. Wipe off the table.
3. Carry the dirty dishes to the sink.
4. Soak them.
5. Wash them.
6. Dry them.
7. Put them away.
8. Clean up the sink.

Sequence 3

1. Go to the washing machine.
2. Put in some clothes.
3. Add some soap.
4. Turn on the washing machine.
5. Take out the clothes.
6. Dry them in the dryer.
7. Put the clothes in a basket.
8. Fold them.

Sequence 4

1. Take the sheets off the bed.
2. Put some clean sheets on it.
3. Take out the garbage.
4. Empty it.
5. Untie the apron strings.
6. Take off the apron.
7. Turn on the television.
8. Lie down on the sofa.

Practice 1

Start each sentence with *If you're cleaning the house, why not.* Omit number 2.
> Example:
> 1. Put on an apron.
> *If you're cleaning the house, why not put on an apron?*

Practice 2

Drop *If you're cleaning the kitchen, why not* and begin each sentence with *Maybe she'll.*
> Example:
> 1. If you're cleaning the kitchen, why not pick up the dirty dishes?
> *Maybe she'll pick up the dirty dishes.*
> 2. If you're cleaning the kitchen, why not wipe off the table?
> 3. If you're cleaning the kitchen, why not carry the dirty dishes to the sink?
> 4. If you're cleaning the kitchen, why not soak the dishes?
> 5. If you're cleaning the kitchen, why not wash the dishes?
> 6. If you're cleaning the kitchen, why not dry the dishes?
> 7. If you're cleaning the kitchen, why not put the dishes away?
> 8. If you're cleaning the kitchen, why not clean up the sink?

Practice 3

Change *Maybe* to *Perhaps*.
Example:
1. Maybe she'll go to the washing machine.
   Perhaps she'll go to the washing machine.
2. Maybe she'll put in some clothes.
3. Maybe she'll add some soap.
4. Maybe she'll turn on the washing machine.
5. Maybe she'll take out the clothes.
6. Maybe she'll dry them in the dryer.
7. Maybe she'll put the clothes in a basket.
8. Maybe she'll fold them.

Practice 4

Drop *Perhaps* and change *will* to *might*.
Example:
1. Perhaps she'll take the sheets off the bed.
   She might take the sheets off the bed.
2. Perhaps she'll put some clean sheets on it.
3. Perhaps she'll take out the garbage.
4. Perhaps she'll empty it.
5. Perhaps she'll untie the apron strings.
6. Perhaps she'll take off the apron.
7. Perhaps she'll turn on the television.
8. Perhaps she'll lie down on the sofa.

CONVERSATION

What do you think you'll do next weekend?

Do you think you'll stay home or go out?
If you go out, where will you go?
If you stay home, do you think you'll clean the house?
If you clean the house, what will you do first?
What will you do after that?

ANSWER KEY

1 MORNING ROUTINE

Practice 1

1. I wake up at seven o'clock.
2. I turn off the alarm clock.
3. I turn on the radio.
4. I listen to the news.
5. I get out of bed.
6. I look out the window.
7. I put on my bathrobe.
8. I walk to the bathroom.

Practice 2

1. I shave with an electric razor every morning.
2. I put on after-shave lotion every morning.
3. I brush my teeth every morning.
4. I comb my hair every morning.
5. I put on my pants every morning.
6. I button my shirt every morning.
7. I stand in front of the mirror every morning.
8. I tie my tie every morning.

Practice 3

1. I don't go into the kitchen every morning.
2. I don't sit down at the table every morning.
3. I don't butter my toast every morning.
4. I don't put salt on my eggs every morning.
5. I don't pour cream in my coffee every morning.
6. I don't put sugar in it every morning.
7. I don't pick up a spoon every morning.
8. I don't stir my coffee every morning.

Practice 4

1. Do you gather your papers together every morning?
2. Do you open your briefcase every morning?
3. Do you put the papers inside every morning?
4. Do you close your briefcase every morning?
5. Do you put on your jacket every morning?
6. Do you straighten your tie every morning?
7. Do you pick up your briefcase every morning?
8. Do you walk out the door every morning?

2   THE TRIP TO WORK

Practice 1

1. Jessica walks down the street every day.
2. She enters the train station every day.
3. She buys a ticket every day.
4. She goes through the turnstile every day.
5. She runs to the platform every day.
6. She gets in line every day.
7. She takes out her handkerchief every day.
8. She wipes her forehead every day.

Practice 2

1. She always gets on the train.
2. She sometimes holds onto a strap.
3. She sometimes sees an empty seat.
4. She sometimes sits down.
5. She sometimes reads the newspaper.
6. She always gives the conductor her ticket.
7. She always gets off the train.
8. She always heads toward the exit.

Practice 3

1. She doesn't always stand at the crosswalk.
2. She doesn't always wait for the green light.
3. She doesn't always cross the street.
4. She doesn't always go into her office building.
5. She doesn't always enter the elevator.
6. She doesn't always push the button.
7. She doesn't always get off on the twelfth floor.
8. She doesn't always walk down the hallway.

Practice 4

1. She doesn't walk into her office on Sundays.
2. She doesn't set her briefcase on her desk on Sundays.
3. She doesn't unlock her desk drawer on Sundays.
4. She doesn't take out any papers on Sundays.
5. She doesn't put on her glasses on Sundays.
6. She doesn't look at the papers on Sundays.
7. She doesn't make phone calls on Sundays.
8. She doesn't talk to clients on Sundays.

3 A BUSINESS LUNCH

Practice 1

1. We meet at ten o'clock.
2. We shake hands.
3. We take out our business cards.
4. We exchange cards.
5. We go into the salesroom.
6. We discuss the sales chart.
7. We look at the sales reports.
8. We go out for lunch.

Practice 2

1 and 2. We get on the elevator and get off on the main floor.
3 and 4. We leave the building and hail a taxi.
5 and 6. We get into the taxi and go to a restaurant.
7 and 8. We pay the taxi driver and get out of the taxi.

Practice 3

1 and 2. We'll walk into the restaurant and find an empty table.
3 and 4. We'll sit down and order some drinks.
5 and 6. We'll make a toast and look at the menu.
7 and 8. We'll call the waiter and order lunch.

Practice 4

1 and 2. After we finish eating, we'll get the bill.
3 and 4. After we take out our wallets, we'll leave a tip for the waiter.
5 and 6. After we go to the cash register, we'll give the cashier some money.
7 and 8. After we get back our change, we'll shake hands.

4   AFTER WORK

Practice 1

1. She always leaves the office at five o'clock.
2. She always gets on the train.
3. She always gets off at her stop.
4. She always walks to the dry cleaners.
5. She always picks up her dry cleaning.
6. She always walks home.
7. She always gets her mail.
8. She always puts the key in the lock.

Practice 2

1. When she gets home from work, she always opens the door.
2. When she gets home from work, she always relaxes in a chair.
3. When she gets home from work, she always reads a letter.
4. When she gets home from work, she always goes into the bedroom.
5. When she gets home from work, she always changes her clothes.
6. When she gets home from work, she always sets the table.
7. When she gets home from work, she always puts some food on the table.
8. When she gets home from work, she always has dinner.

Practice 3

1. When she gets home from work, she sometimes turns on the television.
2. When she gets home from work, she sometimes turns to Channel Two.
3. When she gets home from work, she sometimes watches the news.
4. When she gets home from work, she sometimes changes the channel.
5. When she gets home from work, she sometimes finds a movie.
6. When she gets home from work, she sometimes looks at her watch.
7. When she gets home from work, she sometimes goes into the bathroom.
8. When she gets home from work, she sometimes takes a shower.

Practice 4

1. When does she put on her nightgown?
2. When does she turn back the covers?
3. When does she get into bed?
4. When does she pull up the covers?
5. When does she reach over to the night table?
6. When does she set her alarm clock?
7. When does she turn off the light?
8. When does she go to sleep?

5   COIN-OPERATED MACHINES

Practice 1

1. Now he's walking to a phone booth.
2. Now he's pushing the door open.
3. Now he's stepping inside.
4. Now he's closing the door.
5. Now he's looking in the phone book.
6. Now he's looking for a number.
7. Now he's taking his notebook out.
8. Now he's writing the number down.

Practice 2

1. I'm reaching into my coat pocket.
2. I'm looking at my change.
3. I'm holding a dime.
4. I'm picking up the phone.
5. I'm dropping the coin in the slot.
6. I'm dialing the number.
7. I'm leaning against the glass.
8. I'm hanging up the phone.

Practice 3

1. Are you walking along the street?
2. Are you staring at the cigarette machine?
3. Are you dropping some coins in the machine?
4. Are you pressing a button?
5. Are you picking up the pack of cigarettes?
6. Are you picking up your change?
7. Are you opening the pack?
8. Are you taking out a cigarette?

Practice 4

1. We're going into the subway.
2. We're walking down the steps.
3. We're going to the token booth.
4. We're taking out some coins.
5. We're buying tokens.
6. We're putting the tokens in the slot.
7. We're going through the turnstile.
8. We're waiting on the platform.

6 A VACATION TRIP

Practice 1

1. Mr. Morrison went to the car.
2. He carried his bag.
3. He put the bag in the car.
4. He got in the car.
5. He drove away.
6. He looked at a map.
7. He got onto the expressway.
8. He followed the signs.

Practice 2

1. Did he get off the expressway?
2. Did he arrive at the beach?
3. Did he pull into a service station?
4. Did he ask for directions?
5. Did he drive to the hotel?
6. Did he check into the hotel?
7. Did he give his bag to the bellhop?
8. Did he go to his room?

Practice 3

1. He didn't want to put on his bathing suit.
2. He didn't want to walk to the beach.
3. He didn't want to rent an umbrella.
4. He didn't want to put up the umbrella.
5. He didn't want to spread his towel on the sand.
6. He didn't want to take off his sandals.
7. He didn't want to put on any suntan lotion.
8. He didn't want to stretch out in the sun.

Practice 4

1. Did he want to go swimming?
2. Did he want to play Frisbee?
3. Did he want to eat some sandwiches?
4. Did he want to have a soft drink?
5. Did he want to shake out his towel?
6. Did he want to fold up the towel?
7. Did he want to return the umbrella?
8. Did he want to walk back to the hotel?

7   A BUSINESS MEETING

Practice 1

1. Erik used to work at his desk.
2. He used to look at the clock.
3. He used to pick up his notebook.
4. He used to leave his desk.
5. He used to walk through the office.
6. He used to go to the conference room.
7. He used to sit down at the table.
8. He used to put his elbows on the table.

Practice 2

1. First, he took out a cigarette.
2. Second, he put the cigarette in his mouth.
3. Next, he took out a matchbook.
4. After that, he struck a match.
5. Then, he lit the cigarette.
6. After that, he blew out the match.
7. Then, he took a puff.
8. Finally, he put out the cigarette.

Practice 3

1. Did he ever go to the blackboard?
2. Did he ever pick up a piece of chalk?
3. Did he ever draw a diagram?
4. Did he ever point to the diagram?
5. Did he ever pick up an eraser?
6. Did he ever erase the blackboard?
7. Did he ever put the eraser back?
8. Did he ever return to his seat?

Practice 4

1. He sometimes opened his notebook.
2. He never turned the pages.
3. He sometimes took out his pen.
4. He never took off the cap.
5. He never looked at the blackboard.
6. He never copied any notes.
7. He always closed his notebook.
8. He always left the room.

8   A PARTY

Practice 1

1 and 2. After Mr. and Mrs. Morrison checked the address, they walked up the steps.
3 and 4. After they entered the building, they told the doorman their names.
5 and 6. After they walked into the lobby, they walked up one flight of stairs.
7 and 8. After they looked at the name on the door, they rang the bell.

Practice 2

1 and 2. After saying hello to the host, they took off their coats.
3 and 4. After giving their coats to the hostess, they saw a friend.
5 and 6. After going over to her, they chatted for a few minutes.
7 and 8. After meeting the other guests, they talked with them.

Practice 3

1 and 2. During the party, they went to the punch bowl and filled their glasses.
3 and 4. During the party, they helped themselves to some crackers and put some cheese on them.
5 and 6. During the party, they took some potato chips and sat down on the sofa.
7 and 8. During the party, they drank some punch and listened to music.

Practice 4

1, 2, and 3. After looking at the clock, they got up off the sofa and walked over to the hostess.
4, 5, and 6. After getting their coats from her, they put on their coats (put them on) and said good-bye to the guests.
7, 8, and 9. After thanking the host and hostess, they left the party and . . .

9   A LETTER

Practice 1

1. Jessica has walked into her room.
2. She has walked over to her desk.
3. She has pulled back the chair.
4. She has sat down on the chair.
5. She has opened the drawer.
6. She has reached inside.
7. She has taken out a pen.
8. She has taken out some paper.

Practice 2

1. Has she started to write?
2. Has she written some more?
3. Has she run out of ink?
4. Has she thrown the pen away?
5. Has she looked in the drawer?
6. Has she found another pen?
7. Has she finished writing the letter?
8. Has she signed her name?

Practice 3

1. She hasn't taken out an envelope yet.
2. She hasn't folded the letter yet.
3. She hasn't opened the envelope yet.
4. She hasn't put the letter in yet.
5. She hasn't licked the flap yet.
6. She hasn't sealed the envelope yet.
7. She hasn't addressed the envelope yet.
8. She hasn't put the letter in her pocket yet.

Practice 4

1. I haven't closed the drawer yet.
2. I haven't gotten up from the desk yet.
3. I haven't left the building yet.
4. I haven't walked to the post office yet.
5. I haven't bought a stamp yet.
6. I haven't wet the stamp yet.
7. I haven't stuck the stamp on the envelope yet.
8. I haven't dropped the letter in the mailbox yet.

10   A CLOTHING STORE

Practice 1

1. Erik decided to take a walk.
2. He decided to stop at a men's clothing store.
3. He decided to look in the window.
4. He decided to look at a sports jacket.
5. He decided to go inside the store.
6. He decided to go to the sports jacket section.
7. He decided to reach for a sports jacket.
8. He decided to take it off the rack.

Practice 2

1. He had to look at the label.
2. He had to check the size.
3. He had to try on the sports jacket.
4. He had to move his shoulders.
5. He had to look in the mirror.
6. He had to check the front.
7. He had to turn around.
8. He had to check the back.

Practice 3

1. Did he have to take off the jacket?
2. Did he have to put it on a hanger?
3. Did he have to hang the jacket on the rack?
4. Did he have to find another one?
5. Did he have to put it on?
6. Did he have to check the fit?
7. Did he have to take the jacket to the sales counter?
8. Did he have to call a clerk?

Practice 4

1. He didn't want to hand the jacket to the clerk but he had to.
2. He didn't want to reach into his wallet but he had to.
3. He didn't want to take out a credit card but he had to.
4. He didn't want to hand the card to the clerk but he had to.
5. He didn't want to sign his name but he had to.
6. He didn't want to get a receipt but he had to.
7. He didn't want to pick up the bag but he had to.
8. He didn't want to walk out the door but he had to.

11 A FOOD STORE

Practice 1

1. We'll drive into the parking lot.
2. We'll park the car.
3. We'll walk into the supermarket.
4. We'll go through the turnstile.
5. We'll get a shopping cart.
6. We'll check our grocery list.
7. We'll walk down the aisle.
8. We'll go to the meat section.

Practice 2

1. Let's look at a steak.
2. Let's examine it carefully.
3. Let's look at the price.
4. Let's put it back.
5. Let's pick up a package of hamburger meat.
6. Let's check the price.
7. Let's take another package of hamburger meat.
8. Let's put the packages into the shopping cart.

Practice 3

1. How about stopping at the produce section?
2. How about picking out some tomatoes?
3. How about having them weighed?
4. How about selecting a head of lettuce?
5. How about pushing the cart down the aisle?
6. How about putting some hamburger buns into the shopping cart?
7. How about getting some napkins?
8. How about taking a six-pack of soda?

Practice 4

1. We're going to go to the check-out counter.
2. We're going to wait on line.
3. We're going to put our groceries on the counter.
4. We're going to watch the cashier ring up the bill.
5. We're going to look at the receipt.
6. We're going to pay the bill.
7. We're going to pick up our shopping bags.
8. We're going to carry them out of the store.

12　A DOCTOR'S OFFICE

Practice 1

3. He should make a phone call.
4. He should call the doctor's office.
5. He should talk to a nurse.
6. He should make an appointment.
7. He should go to the doctor's office.

Practice 2

1. Please wait in the waiting room.
2. Please look at a magazine.
3. Please go into the examination room.
4. Please explain what's wrong.
5. Please roll up your sleeve for a test.
6. Please hold out your arm to the doctor.
7. Please roll down your sleeve.
8. Please put your arm down.

Practice 3

1 and 2. Could you take the thermometer from the doctor and put it in your mouth.
3 and 4. Could you take it out and give it to the doctor.
5 and 6. Could you open your mouth and stick out your tongue.
7 and 8. Could you say, "A-a-ahh-h" and close your mouth.

Practice 4

1 and 2. You can unbutton your shirt and take it off now.
3 and 4. You can lie down on the table and be examined by the doctor now.
5 and 6. You can get up off the table and get your shot now.
7 and 8. You can put on your shirt and tuck it in now.

13 COOKING DINNER

Practice 1

1. You go to the kitchen.
2. You open the cupboard.
3. You put some things on the table.
4. You put some butter in a pan.
5. You tap an egg on the table.
6. You break the egg in a bowl.
7. You throw away the shell.
8. You beat the eggs.

Practice 2

1. You should pick up an onion.
2. You should peel it.
3. You should cut the onion into small pieces.
4. You should add it to the eggs.
5. You should reach for a green pepper.
6. You should cut off the top.
7. You should cut out the center.
8. You should clean out the seeds.

Practice 3

1. After that, chop up the pepper.
2. Next, put it in with the eggs.
3. Then, unwrap some ham.
4. After that, slice the ham into strips.
5. Next, drop the ham into the bowl.
6. Then, reach for a spoon.
7. After that, stir the eggs.
8. Finally, wipe off your hands.

Practice 4

1. And then put the pan on the stove.
2. And then turn on the gas.
3. And then turn down the flame.
4. And then pick up the bowl.
5. And then pour the eggs into the pan.
6. And then turn the eggs over.
7. And then lift the eggs out of the pan.
8. And then put the eggs on a plate.

14   A FLAT TIRE

Practice 1

1. I get into the car.
2. I move the seat back.
3. I shut the door.
4. I fasten the seat belt.
5. I clean the mirror.
6. I adjust it.
7. I take out my key.
8. I put the key into the ignition.

Practice 2

1. I have to put my foot on the clutch.
2. I have to step on the brake.
3. I have to turn the key.
4. I have to shift into reverse.
5. I have to look behind me.
6. I have to release the clutch.
7. I have to step on the gas.
8. I have to back up.

Practice 3

1. I'll have to step on the brake.
2. I'll have to get out of the car.
3. I'll have to examine the flat tire.
4. I'll have to find the hole in it.
5. I'll have to open the trunk.
6. I'll have to take out the jack.
7. I'll have to jack up the car.
8. I'll have to take off the wheel.

Practice 4

1. I'm going to take out the spare.
2. I'm going to put it on.
3. I'm going to screw on the nuts.
4. I'm going to tighten them.
5. I'm going to put on the hubcap.
6. I'm going to put the flat tire in the trunk.
7. I'm going to close the trunk.
8. I'm going to drive to a service station.

15   HOUSE CLEANING

Practice 1

1. If you're cleaning the house, why not put on an apron?
3. If you're cleaning the house, why not wash the windows?
4. If you're cleaning the house, why not dust the furniture?
5. If you're cleaning the house, why not plug in the vacuum cleaner?
6. If you're cleaning the house, why not vacuum the floor?
7. If you're cleaning the house, why not water the plants?
8. If you're cleaning the house, why not straighten the pictures?

Practice 2

1. Maybe she'll pick up the dirty dishes.
2. Maybe she'll wipe off the table.
3. Maybe she'll carry the dirty dishes to the sink.
4. Maybe she'll soak the dishes.
5. Maybe she'll wash the dishes.
6. Maybe she'll dry the dishes.
7. Maybe she'll put the dishes away.
8. Maybe she'll clean up the sink.

Practice 3

1. Perhaps she'll go to the washing machine.
2. Perhaps she'll put in some clothes.
3. Perhaps she'll add some soap.
4. Perhaps she'll turn on the washing machine.
5. Perhaps she'll take out the clothes.
6. Perhaps she'll dry them in the dryer.
7. Perhaps she'll put the clothes in a basket.
8. Perhaps she'll fold them.

Practice 4

1. She might take the sheets off the bed.
2. She might put some clean sheets on it.
3. She might take out the garbage.
4. She might empty it.
5. She might untie the apron strings.
6. She might take off the apron.
7. She might turn on the television.
8. She might lie down on the sofa.